SLEEPING WITH MOSCOW

By Anatole Verbitzky and Dick Adler

SHAPOLSKY PUBLISHERS
New York

A Shapolsky Book
Published by Shapolsky Publishers

For any additional information, contact:
Shapolsky Publishers, Inc., 56 East 11th Street, New York, NY 10003

10 9 8 7 6 5 4 3 2 1

Library of Congress Cataloging-in-Publication Data:
Verbitzky, Anatole, 1927-
Sleeping with Moscow

1. Ogorodnikov, Svetalana. 2. Ogorodnikov, Nikolai. 3. Miller, Richard W. 4. Spies . Soviet Union . Biography. 5. Spies . United States . Biography. 6. Espionage . Soviet Union . History . 20th century. 7. Espionage . United States . History . 20th century. 8. United States. Federal Bureau of Investigation.
I. Adler, Dick, 1937— II. Title.
UB271.R920378 1987 327.1'2'0922 [B] 87—9692

ISBN 0-933503-07-5

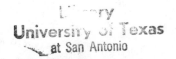

TABLE OF CONTENTS

TABLE OF CONTENTS

PREFACE

This is the story of what happened when two of the most inept Russian spies in the world met one of America's dumbest FBI agents. As of December 1986, all three are in federal prisons across the country, doing time as convicted spies for Russia. The former FBI man, forty-nine-year-old Richard W. Miller—the first FBI agent ever convicted of espionage—is serving his sentence of two life terms plus fifty years in a Minnesota prison. Svetlana Ogorodnikova, the thirty-six-year-old Russian woman accused of being Miller's lover and convicted of helping him with his spying, is in jail in Pleasanton, California, sentenced to eighteen years after she pleaded guilty. And Svetlana's husband, Nikolai Ogorodnikov, a fifty-three-year-old former Kiev taxi driver and Los Angeles meat cutter who pleaded guilty to aiding his wife, is serving his eight-year sentence in Phoenix, Arizona. Other victims in the case, such as Miller's wife and eight children and the Ogorodnikov's fourteen-year-old son, Matthew, are being punished in other ways.

Sleeping With Moscow is the story of all three of these people, but it is told primarily from the viewpoint of Nikolai Ogorodnikov—a man who both sides agree was the least guilty of the three principals. But who exactly is Nikolai Ogorodnikov? Is he the pathetic father, the almost totally innocent victim of his wife's drunken and dangerous behavior, as he implies? Is he, as the prosecution pictures him, a basically immoral man who let his wife lead him into trouble and then never tried

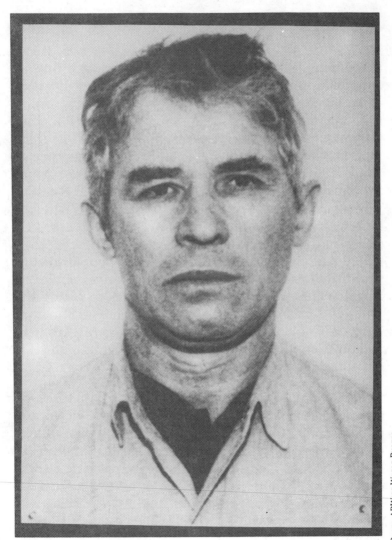

to get out? Or does the truth lie somewhere in between these two positions—in those dark areas of human weakness that we never know about until it's almost too late?

Santa Monica, California
April 1987

Nikolai Ogorodnikov's dream of a new start in the United States was dashed when he was sentenced to seven years in jail—as a spy for the Soviet Union.

Chapter 1

INTO THE NET

I F you happened to be having dinner at a fancy cafeteria called Café Casino, looking out over the Pacific Ocean in Santa Monica, California, on September 13, 1984, seated among the eager tourists and the glossy residents you might have noticed an unusual couple. He was a portly man in his late forties in a rumpled polyester sports jacket, big and bland and genial but also on this occasion definitely ill at ease. She was a small, attractive, foxy blonde woman a dozen years younger, who spoke with a heavy accent, was full of nervous energy, and was clearly in control of the situation.

You could also have spotted this couple on September 12 and 26 of that same year in the parking lot of the Little League baseball field on Sepulveda Boulevard, just south of the Federal Building on Wilshire Boulevard in the Los Angeles suburb of Westwood. The meeting on September 12, in the woman's 1983 Mercury Lynx automobile, was especially noteworthy. It lasted more than four hours.

And if you had been taking a stroll through the leafy neighborhood surrounding the Russian Consulate on

Green Street in San Francisco on August 25, 1984, you might have seen this same couple: he waiting nervously in a restaurant nearby, she entering the well-guarded cream-and-gray building and coming out to join him some hours later.

The portly man and the foxy woman had several other furtive meetings during August and September of 1984: on the beach in Malibu, at her shabby apartment on Gardner Street in Hollywood, at his seedy weekday residence on Josephine Street in the suburb of Lynwood. What moves all of these encounters out of the area of routine salacious interest is not that the portly man, Richard W. Miller, had a wife and eight children living down in Bonsall, near San Diego, nor that the foxy woman, Svetlana Ogorodnikova, had a thirteen-year-old son and a husband named Nikolai who worked as a meat-packer. What makes them of historical importance is that he was an FBI agent and she was a Russian spy.

When Miller and the Ogorodnikovs were arrested in October of 1984, it was the little details that fascinated the world's press. The fact that Miller had been reprimanded by the FBI for selling Amway products out of the back of his official car, for example. Or that Ogorodnikova, supposedly a KGB agent, even possibly a major, was receiving monthly welfare checks from Los Angeles County. Or that part of Miller's reward for spying was supposed to be a $675 Burberry trench coat—the one with all those zippers and buckles and rings for holding hand grenades. Or, most suprising of all, the fact that after twenty years as an FBI agent, Miller never seemed to have noticed that he was being tailed and bugged and surveilled daily by dozens of his colleagues for over a month before his arrest.

From the outside, at least before his fall from grace, Richard William Miller — "R.W." to his friends — might have been a Norman Rockwell model of the all-American FBI man and father. A dutiful Mormon, he grew up in the Los Angeles suburb of Lynwood, attended Compton Junior College from 1955 to 1957, then graduated from Brigham Young University in 1963, with degrees in Spanish and English. At one time Miller wanted to become a Spanish teacher, but a job offer from the FBI right after college changed all that. He married a fellow Mormon, Paula Gonzalez, and settled down to raise eight children — the oldest now twenty-one and studying to be a Mormon missionary in Guatemala, the youngest just four. He served his church as a Sunday school teacher and home visitor; he coached Little League baseball; he helped out at a special school for the hearing impaired where his eighteen-year-old son Drew was a student.

Miller's surface image was just about as far as you can get from the one projected by Nikolai and Svetlana Ogorodnikov. The Russian couple definitely appeared to be losers in the game of life. In Kiev he had been a taxi driver with a prison record who married a woman seventeen years younger because she was pregnant. She had a family history of alcoholism and worked occasionally as a janitor. In 1973, because Nikolai's family was Jewish, they managed to get exit visas to Israel but came to America instead. But unlike most recent Russian immigrants, their lives hadn't improved very much. He got a job cutting meat for $400 a week at a plant in Vernon; she claimed to be working part-time as a nurse's aide, although nobody else remembers her doing it for longer than a week. They lived with their son, Matthew, in a shabby one-bedroom apartment in a transient section of Hollywood. Their only visible luxury was the Mercury Lynx, paid for out of the money they made by filing several personal injury suits. One was against a driver who said the Ogorodnikovs had backed into his car, but his insurance company decided it was cheaper to settle than fight. Another suit was against a dentist who, Svetlana claimed, hadn't anchored a bridge properly. He, too, elected to pay a small amount rather than go to court. Also unlike most recent Russian immigrants, Nikolai and Svetlana were loudly and openly pro-Soviet and anti-American — so much so that they were shunned by most of Los Angeles's large Russian community. In 1982, upset by Svetlana's drinking and immoral behavior, Nikolai filed for separation — even though the Ogorodnikovs continued to live together under the same roof.

But those were just the outward appearances. In both cases, anyone scratching below the surface could have found curious and disturbing contradictions. Miller, for example, didn't really fit the picture of efficiency or glamour that the FBI likes to project. Most of his career consisted of years of routine work, performed with no special skill. He had served in San Antonio, New York, Puerto Rico, and Florida before coming back home to California. As the agent in charge of the Bureau's small office in Riverside, he once helped recover a truckload of stolen candy — earning a rare commendation. This was balanced by repeated warnings, reprimands and even a short suspension for failing to keep his weight down, and for getting caught moonlighting Amway products out of his FBI car.

Miller's fellow agents saw him as a friendly boob at best, a disgrace to his badge at worst. When he was transferred into a soft job in the counterintelligence department in 1981, there were growls of protest from other agents. Many of them put the promotion down to special treatment on the part of the FBI's "Old Mormon Network." The two top agents in Los Angeles, Richard T. Bretzing and P. Bryce Christensen, were Mormons, and there had been charges of favoritism toward fellow Mormons in the past.

But the new assignment, in the Los Angeles office, wasn't really glamorous — he monitored and logged electronic surveillance in a windowless back room — and it didn't really make Miller's life any easier. The distance from his home in Bonsall forced him to spend weeknights in the now sparsely-furnished and generally dilapidated house in the working-class neighborhood of Lynwood where he had grown up. This expense added to the other financial pressures of raising a large family on a salary of $45,000 a year led Miller into a series of failed financial schemes. One was a plunge, with his father-in-law, into avocado farming — the Californian agricultural equivalent of being an Amway dealer. He also admitted later to routinely supplying a private detective with FBI data in return for small payments, and to cheating his wife's uncle by selling some foot massagers the man had invented and pocketing all of the money. Even his record as a Mormon was stained. Miller was excommunicated in 1984 after being caught in an extramarital affair with another Mormon.

As for the Ogorodnikovs, the picture of them as just a pair of conniving émigré stumblebums is somewhat shaken by evidence of what seems to be a certain sudden affluence, and access to special privilege. Despite their low-rent housing, Svetlana always appeared to have plenty of money for entertainment and travel, and once offered a lawyer a large sum to help locate a top Russian defector. She and Nikolai were given permission to show Russian films supplied by the Consulate in San Francisco at a Los Angeles theater and keep a share of the proceeds, even though neither had any previous experience in this kind of venture. Mischa Makarian, the owner of Mischa's, a Russian restaurant and cabaret on Sunset Boulevard, knew her as a regular customer. "She brought in interesting guests — people from the Consulate in San Francisco, people from the Soviet cinema industry looking for American distributors," he recalls. "She always paid her way, and tipped well." The Ogorodnikovs' son spent several summer sessions at an Artek camp in Russia — a privilege not usually granted to the children of Jewish emigrants. And both Svetlana and Nikolai flew from Los Angeles to Russia several times — an expensive trip requiring the kind of money and resourcefulness not often found in the average meat cutter earning $20,000 a year.

All of these contradictions came into play when Richard Miller met Svetlana Ogorodnikova for the first time in May of 1984. According to Miller, Svetlana called the FBI office and said that she could give them information on the Russian émigré community in Los Angeles. He followed up and arranged a meeting. Miller at that point didn't know, or at least pushed to the back of his mind, that Svetlana had been meeting with an FBI counterintelligence agent named John Hunt since 1980. According to Svetlana (although Hunt denied it), they had been lovers, and Hunt once arranged and paid for an abortion. Miller's official .story, the one he would stick to during three different trials, was that he saw Svetlana as a chance to redeem himself. By putting the Russian woman to work for him as a double agent, he would prove to all the doubters that inside his overweight body beat the heart of a true FBI man.

It was at their second meeting, the very next day, that Miller and Svetlana had sex in the back seat of her car, parked on the beach in Malibu. (Indeed, according to Miller, they had sex on virtually every occasion they were together. He said that Svetlana was quite passive about the sex, telling investigators later that her attitude was, "Well, if that's what you want, okay.") Miller found himself confiding his financial and work problems to her, and she listened and responded sympathetically. On their fourth or fifth date, in August, after she came back from a trip to Russia, that sympathy turned into an offer of help.

"While at a restaurant in Malibu," Miller later recalled, "Svetlana became very serious and asked me if I wanted to work with the KGB. She said I could make a lot of money if I did that. I told her that I was not interested. However, if I ever did do something like that, it would have to be for a lot of money, like one or two million dollars, because if I was caught I would lose my job and everything."

A few days later, after a particularly alcoholic dinner, Svetlana took Miller to her apartment and introduced him to a man she called Nikolai Wolfson, the KGB's moneyman in the Los Angeles area. According to Miller's testimony later, Wolfson took him for a walk around the block and asked him how much he needed to supply Svetlana with secret FBI documents. Miller dropped his "one or two million dollars" down to a more realistic $50,000 in gold and $15,000 in cash; Wolfson assured him that this would be "no problem." Checking the FBI files the next morning, Miller said that he was surprised to discover that Wolfson was really Nikolai Ogorodnikov.

The discovery didn't stop him. Nine days later, Miller and Svetlana were on their way to San Francisco, in her car. It was primarily a pleasure trip, with stops for sex and sleep at motels along the way. According to the statement that Miller made to his superiors after his arrest in October — the one that he and his lawyers called an "explanation" but the FBI labeled a "confession" — Svetlana told him on the trip that she was a major in the KGB. Nobody but a few newspapers ever took this statement seriously, and none of the subsequent charges ever mentioned it. United States Attorney Robert Bonner said at the time of the arrests, "I think you are going to have to draw your own inferences about the kinds of agents Svetlana and Nikolai are."

When they arrived in San Francisco, Svetlana asked for Miller's black leather case containing his badge and FBI identification card, to take into the Russian Consulate to prove that he was the real thing. Miller handed her the case; she dropped him off at a nearby restaurant while she went back to the Consulate to deliver several film canisters. Inside one of the canisters, according to the FBI, was a photocopy of a twenty-four-page FBI document classified "Secret" and titled *Reporting Guidance: Foreign Intelligence Information*. They later charged Miller with copying the document on the FBI's own machine, taking the copy home to Lynwood, then delivering it to Svetlana on their trip.

17

According to the FBI, the booklet was a significant piece of intelligence. "Discovery of this document would give the KGB a detailed picture of FBI and U.S. intelligence activities, techniques and requirements," insisted P. Bryce Christensen. Other FBI agents weren't so sure. "The word 'trivial' would be overstating its importance," said one at the time. "It was just a list of things for an agent to remember when dealing with foreigners."

It was shortly after the trip to San Francisco that things began to happen thick and fast for Miller and the Ogorodnikovs. Although the FBI never announced it officially, they had been keeping many Russian Consulates under electronic surveillance, checking the identities of people who visited them. On September 1, 1984, a week after Svetlana's visit, the FBI got a court order and began tapping the Ogorodnikovs' Hollywood phone. Soon after that, agents began watching the Gardner Street apartment. In a neighborhood where new cars and men in business suits are rare, they managed to go about their business for a month without being noticed. Fully expecting to catch some KGB colonel masking as a diplomat, the FBI surveillance team soon began to realize that they were on to something even more dangerous — one of their agents who appeared to have sold out.

FBI surveillance logs and edited transcripts of wiretaps tell the next part of the story better than any novelist or screenwriter could. The file was labeled "Whipworm" by the Bureau, after an insidious internal parasite, and contained entries such as these:

— "On Tuesday, September 11, at 7:54 P.M., an unknown male placed a call to Svetlana Ogorodnikova at her residence. The conversation began in English, but both

18

parties switched to Russian once the initial contact was made.

"Unknown Caller: 'I am calling you on behalf of your aquaintances. . .with whom you had occasion to meet this last summer. Well, now, Svetlana, your friends would like to propose that you, together with your friend, by the means with which you are already familiar, both go to see them. All expenses will be reimbursed. Also, your friend should bring everything he can, as was discussed in the special house.'

"At 11:12 P.M., a call was placed by Svetlana Ogorodnikova to Richard W. Miller. She initiated conversation to arrange for a meeting between them, which was set for the following day."

—"On September 12, at 5:31 P.M., an FBI surveillance team observed Miller leave the Los Angeles office of the FBI, carrying a dark briefcase, and drive in his personal vehicle to a parking lot of a park located on Sepulveda Boulevard south of the Federal Building, 11000 Wilshire Boulevard., Los Angeles. At 5:57 P.M., an automobile driven by Svetlana Ogorodnikova arrived. Miller exited his vehicle carrying a legal-sized envelope, entered the passenger side of Ogorodnikova's vehicle and handed the envelope to Ogorodnikova. Svetlana Ogorodnikova and Miller remained together until 10:09 P.M., when she departed in her vehicle."

This four-hour meeting was just one of several long sessions that Miller and Svetlana had over the next two weeks — all under the watchful and patient surveillance of his FBI colleagues. The purpose of these meetings, aside from the sex that was recorded on audio and video tape, was to finalize the details of a trip they were to make together so that Svetlana could introduce Miller to someone higher up in the Soviet espionage hierarchy. Miller at first insisted that the meeting be in Mexico, and that was the destination he put down when he applied for a passport on September 21 — listing his occupation as "translator." Miller even made things easy for his tails by using the passport office in the Federal Building, just a few floors below his own office.

But Mexico was too close for Svetlana's "Unknown Caller," later identified by the FBI as Aleksandr Grishin, the vice consul at the Russian Consulate in San Francisco. Grishin, named by the United States Government as an unindicted co-conspirator in the case against Miller and the Ogorodnikovs, insisted that the meeting take place in Warsaw or at least Vienna, so Svetlana made the travel arrangements through the Beverly International Travel Agency in Beverly Hills. She and Miller were to fly from Los Angeles to Vienna on October 9, then return to Los Angeles by way of Switzerland on October 14. The FBI assumed that the $4,000 for the tickets came from a "large wad of bills," which an agent observed Nikolai Ogorodnikov receiving from a Bank of America teller in San Francisco on September 24, not long after he visited the Russian Consulate carrying a gray film canister. But Nikolai's lawyers were able to show later that the "large wad" was probably the change from a $20 withdrawal from his own account, which he had made to pay for the bus back to the airport.

September 26 was a big day for Miller, the Day of the Burberry. He and Svetlana visited several men's stores, shopping for clothes for his trip to Vienna. One of the items selected was a size 50 Burberry trench coat, not much use in Los Angeles in September but good protection against the damp and chill of autumn in Austria. Svetlana put a hold on the $675 coat, and said she would pick it up in a day or two. But Miller never got to wear his expensive trench coat; it was seized by the FBI from the store and held as evidence.

After the shopping spree, Miller and Svetlana drove to their favorite park behind the Federal Building, where they began to behave rather oddly. According to the FBI surveillance log, they "exited her vehicle and walked around the perimeter of the park three times before returning to her vehicle. Miller then opened the trunk of Ogorodnikova's vehicle and removed a small suitcase that he then placed in the trunk of his own vehicle. Then the two resumed walking around the park."

The FBI's Bryce Christensen offered this explanation of their behavior in a footnote: "Based on my experience in prior cases, I believe it is common procedure for individuals involved in hostile intelligence activities to take steps to minimize the possibility that sensitive conversations might be identified or intercepted by counterintelligence services. One technique commonly used is to conduct sensitive conversations in an outside public environment while walking in a random fashion. That technique significantly reduces the fear of being detected by electronic surveillance."

That night, Miller drove to the house on Josephine Street in Lynwood where he slept during the week. Scattered around the sparsely furnished house were several original documents from FBI files — documents that Miller had taken out without signing for them. (They were found there later by FBI agents after Miller gave them a consent-to-search form.) Miller was definitely feeling nervous, ill-at-ease today. According to his own statement and later testimony, he had finally realized that he might be getting in over his head — that trying to trap Svetlana by getting her to introduce him to a top KGB or GRU (Soviet Military Intelligence) officer in Vienna was beyond his own limited experience and abilities as an FBI agent. The FBI said later that Miller was nervous because he had spotted one of his fellow agents watching him from a car in the Sepulveda parking lot, and knew the game was up.

Whatever his motives, Miller finally decided to put his cards on the table and ask the Bureau for help. After a restless night, he drove back into Westwood and told his superiors everything: how he had met Svetlana, how he had dangled hints about being ready to sell out, how he had arranged things so that she would wind up working as a double agent for him. But instead of praising him for his initiative and offering to help, his FBI colleagues proceeded to grill Miller like a split trout for the next five days. They alternated teams of counter-intelligence agents with polygraph experts as they worked to rip his story apart.

It was at this time, Miller's lawyers would later charge, that the Old Mormon Network began to work against him. They claimed that Richard Bretzing, the FBI chief agent in Los Angeles, used his position as a bishop in the Mormon Church to coerce a confession from Miller by reciting "the five steps of the process," a Mormon method for persons to admit all their sins as a first step toward forgiveness. Bretzing denied the charge, saying that when he asked Miller to "repent," he was speaking only as his boss, not as a religious leader. Bretzing said of his meeting on September 29 with Miller, "I suggested to him that while he probably recognized the legal, social, and moral ramifications of the activities about which he was interviewed, I wondered if he had considered the spiritual ramifications. I reminded him of the beliefs he had once held that included the need to repent when one transgressed a law or offended someone. I reminded him that this belief stipulated the need not only for confession to the offended parties but for restitution for the wrongful act."

Miller's lawyers said that Bretzing's statement proved their contention that Miller's "confession" was obtained by coercion. They pointed to a statement by Bryce Christensen that while he was driving Miller home after an interview session, "Miller expressed feelings of total exhaustion and frustration. He stated that he was developing the impression that his interviewers were attempting to make him believe he did something he did not recall doing. He indicated he was so exhausted by the interview process that he sometimes felt that he was ready to admit anything just to get the process over with."

While Miller was being grilled by his employers, the tension level was also running high at the apartment of Nikolai and Svetlana Ogorodnikov. FBI surveillance logs show plenty of telephone activity during those five days: twenty-three unanswered calls from Svetlana's phone to Miller's office and to his Lynwood number.

Finally, on October 2, instead of sending him off to Vienna with expert advice on how to turn a sexy Soviet spy into a double agent, the FBI fired Richard Miller and arrested him for espionage. At the same time, a team of

FBI agents crept up to the Ogorodnikovs' apartment at midnight and arrested Svetlana and Nikolai. He was found to be holding a loaded pistol; an agent said later that it was lucky he hadn't been shot.

So the three people whose lives had seemed so far apart came together at last — on a United States Government indictment for espionage.

Chapter 2

OUT OF THE FRYING PAN

Nikolai visiting the San Diego Zoo

THAT October night in 1984 wasn't the first time Nikolai had been arrested and put in jail. The Germans had locked him up in Grunewald in 1945, a boy soldier fighting with the Russian Army, after he was captured during World War II. Luckily, he thought fast; he lied and told the Germans that his name was not Wolfson — the Jewish name he was born with — but Ogorodnikov, which means "to fence in," or else he might have wound up in another kind of camp. When he got back to Russia, he spent some time in a military prison for not returning his army rifle. And after the war, back in his native Kiev, there were other scrapes with the law. "I served time in a KGB prison because they saw me going into the American and Canadian embassies," Nikolai says. "There was also some problem with trying to change dollars when my uncle came over from America. And there was a hit-and-run accident when I ran over a teenage boy."

During one of his prison stays, Nikolai remembers meeting a man who was accused of espionage because he had sent some technical reports of minor importance

28

to be published in Finland and Sweden. "Even though he denied that he was a spy, he was fascinated·by the subject, and knew by heart almost the entire history of espionage. Realizing that I, too, was very interested, he would talk for hours about the great spies of history, and how each major country used its spies. Little did I realize that one day I myself might become part of somebody else's prison story."

Even though he had some technical training as an electrician, Nikolai found that with his prison record good jobs were hard to find. He worked as a taxi driver in Kiev, planning to move to Riga or some other city where his record might not be known. He married, fathered a daughter, got divorced. Then, in 1967, he met the woman who would be his downfall.

"Svetlana wasn't even eighteen when we started going out, and I was already thirty-five," Nikolai says. "What she saw in me I don't know, although in those days I looked younger and was always interested in a good time. People warned me against her; they said she had a drinking problem which ran in her family. Certainly I knew that her father had died of drink, but I didn't pay much attention. Before I knew it, she was pregnant and we got married.

"Things didn't look too bright for us, until my uncle from America came on one of his regular visits. His name was Samuel Wolfson, although he called himself Sam Wolf in Los Angeles, where he owned a shoe factory. On this visit, he offered to help me get a visa to leave Russia. There was a big wave of Jewish immigration going on; perhaps we would have to stop first in Israel, but Uncle Sam said he'd get us to Los Angeles soon.

"So it was that in 1973, after waiting six months for our visas, Svetlana and I and our baby son, Matvey — he quickly became Matthew in America — left Kiev for Vienna, on our way to Israel. At the Vienna airport, Svetlana went upstairs to smoke a cigarette and she met a woman who knew her way around. 'Why go to Israel when your husband has relatives in America?' she told her. 'Go see this guy I know over at the desk and tell him your story; you'll be on your way to Los Angeles in no time!'

"She turned out to be right. We got our tickets changed, flew to New York and then on to Los Angeles, where we headed directly for Uncle Sam's house. I knew he'd let us stay with him until I could get a job and find a place of our own.

"But our luck had run out. My Uncle Sam had died the week before, and his wife, my aunt, who I had never met, wasn't in the mood for visiting relatives. She didn't invite us in — even after I told her we had come six thousand miles because my uncle had promised to help us. 'You want to talk to your uncle?' she said. 'He's at the Jewish Cemetery — grave number 812! I know nothing about any promises. Now leave me alone; I'm a sick woman myself.' To get rid of us, she counted out a hundred dollars in ten-dollar bills, then closed her door on us.

"So we had to start our glamorous new life in America literally from nothing. At first, some help was given to us by an organization that looks after newly-arrived Soviet immigrants, but that soon ran out. I took any job I could: I worked as a night watchman in a supermarket,

Svetlana Ogorodnikov

as a loader in a warehouse, on construction jobs where you didn't have to belong to a union. Then, about six months after we arrived, I was lucky enough to meet someone who told me of an opening in a meat-packing plant in Vernon. I started there right away, and was in the same job until I was arrested.

"Things began to improve. My son was growing up, we had bought a car and opened a bank account. True, our apartment on Gardner Street wasn't fancy, but it was cheap — and as a Russian I didn't expect to live in a mansion in Beverly Hills. I was happy, but Svetlana — with her peculiar taste for adventure — wanted more."

It wasn't long after they arrived and set themselves up in Hollywood that Svetlana and Nikolai began to be noticed by the thirty thousand other Russian émigrés in Los Angeles. "In the beginning, she said she was promoting Soviet-American cultural relations," recalls Mischa Makarian, whose restaurant and cabaret, Mischa's, on Sunset Boulevard, is a popular gathering place for the Russian community. "But through the years I saw that the cultural relations were all one-sided. She wasn't doing anything to promote America. She was bringing in Soviet magazines and giving them to people, leaving leaflets promoting Soviet films on my bar.

"But one thing she did was so bad that everybody really cut her off," Makarian continues. "She was bringing her son to our Russian Orthodox Church on Saturdays, and there was this family that had had a tragedy. There were six children, and the oldest was shot to death. The family was very low in spirits, and it was at this time that Svetlana approached them, told them how life back in the Soviet Union was so much better than here, there was so much less violence, and actually persuaded the whole family to move back to Russia! After that, the other members of the church threw her out."

Alexander Polovets, the editor and publisher of the Russian-language weekly *Almanac Panorama*, first had occasion to write about Nikolai and Svetlana in 1980, after they were involved in arranging a concert at the Wilshire Ebell Theater. The show was supposed to have starred several well-known Soviet performers, but actually offered a group of amateurs from the crew of a Russian ship docked in San Pedro. In a letter of thanks in his newspaper, Polovets ironically referred to the couple as "Mr. and Mrs. Podzabornikov" — a Russian pun, since Ogorodnikov means "to fence in" and Podzabornikov means "under the fence," or, in the vernacular, "in the gutter."

Three years later, when some genuine Russian stars gave a concert at Hollywood High School, Polovets spotted Nikolai taking pictures of what he says were anti-Soviet demonstrators outside the building. "He had a camera with a big telephoto lens," Polovets recalls. "I also had my camera with a telephoto lens, so I took a picture of him!" Polovets's picture of Nikolai appeared in magazines and newspapers around the world after his arrest.

"Most people were suspicious of the Ogorodnikovs from the beginning, but some still got sucked in," Polovets says. "For example, at one of their movie shows, they announced that soon they would be selling tickets for a live concert by the great Russian comedian Arkady Raikin. Now, Raikin is like Charlie Chaplin or Bob Hope, very famous, and our people miss him and love him very much. So naturally when the Ogorodnikovs say, 'Give us your names and addresses so we can send you a notice when the tickets go on sale,' many people sign up. I know, and many others know, that this concert will never happen. Raikin is Jewish, he is not allowed to travel, and also he is very sick. But those people who gave their names are soon receiving flyers and Russian propaganda. And who knows what other uses their names and addresses will have?"

A few people in the Russian community still insist that this kind of heavy-handed and obvious behavior by Nikolai and Svetlana was part of a very clever cover to disguise their activities as KGB agents. But most of their fellow Russians think that the Ogorodnikovs weren't smart enough to pull off such a ploy. "What probably happened was that Svetlana got fed up and wanted to work her way back home, and Nikolai agreed to help her," says one community leader. "So she went to the Russian Consulate in San Francisco, where she was told, 'Sure you can go home; all you have to do is perform a few small chores for us as part of the payment.' "

Nikolai denies the existence of any such scheme. "What happened was that Svetlana had a friend named Berta, a talkative woman always looking for adventure," he says. "It was this woman who told her she would introduce her to some Russian friends in San Francisco, at the Consulate. She said they were always looking for people to do them favors, so they could help them in return. At first, Svetlana was afraid to do it; she told me about it, and I said she would have to be crazy to go along with what Berta suggested. But I found out later that Berta kept insisting, and finally Svetlana gave in."

Sometime during this period, either through Berta or on her own, Svetlana also came in contact with John

Hunt, the FBI agent then in charge of keeping an eye on the Russian community in Los Angeles, which was quickly catching up with New York as a center of Soviet immigration. (According to Svetlana's later testimony, she and Hunt almost immediately began a romantic attachment; Hunt promised to divorce his wife and marry her. All through the trials of the Ogorodnikovs and Richard Miller, however, Hunt — who had retired from the FBI shortly before the three were arrested — insisted that his involvement with Svetlana was strictly business.)

Nikolai says that everything came to a head in April of 1980, when Svetlana learned that Soviet diplomats and specialists living in America got to send their children to the Artek camp in the Crimea every summer. "This place was a child's dream — all day long they swim, play, eat the best food, watch movies. And somehow Svetlana got the idea in her head that our boy should go to this dream camp. How was it possible that the son of poor immigrants who had given up their citizenship and were seen as traitors to their homeland could join with the children of ministers and generals? Svetlana was never the type to retreat in front of such difficult questions. When she first told me about it, she said she would tell them that our boy deserved to go to Artek because his grandfather, her father, was a hero of World War II and had also helped to build many big factories. This wasn't quite the truth, but who would check it? Svetlana had always been an expert liar.

"I said she would only make a fool of herself if she went with such a story," Nikolai continues. "Was she really so stupid? Didn't she know that the employees of the Soviet Consulates were mostly top KGB agents? But there was no stopping her. 'What do we have to lose; maybe they'll be touched by my story and let Matvey go to their camp,' was her reply. Three days later, she went to San Francisco. As she told me later, it wasn't easy even getting into the Soviet Consulate. First she needed a pass, which she didn't have. So she called up on the phone and told a secretary that she had to speak urgently with either the consul, Aleksandr Chikvaidze, or the vice consul, Aleksandr Grishin — names she knew from her friend Berta. Finally, she got to speak with Grishin. 'I have some information about Russian immigrants living in Los Angeles which you might be interested in,' she tells him. 'Yes? Okay, I'll leave a pass in your name,' Grishin says.

"This Grishin turned out to be a friendly fellow. He listened carefully to what she had to say, that she could provide a list of certain 'interesting' people living in the Russian community. He asked her to write down her list and also all about herself, an autobiography. She tried to remember the notes she had made about Russians in Los Angeles: this one owns an antique store in Hollywood and sells to movie stars; this one is a journalist who is said to deal in drugs; this old couple are sending back to Russia letters in Yiddish, urging people to emigrate. Grishin took the papers and told her to come back in an hour.

"Svetlana told me that she spent that hour wandering around the streets of San Francisco and worrying how closely they would be checking her life story," Nikolai says. "When she came back, to her great relief Grishin was smiling. 'These aren't bad, but in future we need many more details. By the way, why are you offering us your services? Is it money you want?' Svetlana told me she quickly assured him she wasn't after payment. 'No, what I want is for my son to go to Artek — even for a short visit.' Grishin looked surprised at her request. 'Artek! You've got some nerve, I must say. Do you know how hard it is to get a child into Artek?' Svetlana told him she realized the problem, but would appreciate any help he could give her. 'All right, we'll see. Was there anything else?' Grishin asked. And Svetlana brought up something we had often talked about as a way of making some money. 'All the Russians immigrants are hungry for films from home,' she told him. 'Could you help us get these pictures to show in Los Angeles?' Grishin assured her that he would do his best.

"Before she left, Grishin gave Svetlana some instructions: 'Keep quiet, tell no one about this, not even your husband. Make friends among the Russian immigrants, and tell us not only about bad things but also about people who seem to want to go back home to Russia. And if you ever get to meet any important American officials, people in the military or the police or the government, make it your business to get to be friendly with them.'

"Svetlana told me later that on the flight home she was in agony, wondering what trouble she had let herself in for. But, like everything with her, the worries soon passed. When she told me about the trip, some five or six days later, I exploded and we had a really bad fight. 'You're playing with fire!' I told her. 'Do you think the KGB doesn't know how to deal with liars and smart-asses?' She said, 'What's so terrible? Do you want to be

37

a butcher all your life? All I want is to send Matvey to Artek and to get some films for us.' Soon we were shouting and I was threatening to leave her and get a divorce. It wasn't the first time, or the last. But the thought of being without my boy always stopped me."

Chapter 3

THE NOOSE TIGHTENS

F OR Nikolai, life in America began to take on a definite shape. He would get up early and take the bus to work in Vernon. When he got home, Svetlana was often out, so he fixed supper for Matthew and himself. When Svetlana did come home, there were arguments — she was often drunk and surly. "I had finally stopped trying to talk to her about what she was doing at the Consulate in San Francisco," he says. "I was sick and tired of hearing about how she wasn't doing anything bad by giving the Russians information. But I knew in my heart that she hadn't stopped."

In fact, Svetlana had been very busy, according to documents later filed by the FBI. A Russian woman seeking political asylum in the United States was visited by Svetlana and urged to return to the Soviet Union. Then Svetlana brought two officials from the Soviet Consulate in San Francisco to the woman's apartment, and all three hammered away at the woman, to no avail. Svetlana also once drove Soviet vice consul Viktor Zonov from Los Angeles Airport to a police station in Anaheim to arrange bail for a Russian student

In a happy mood, Los Angeles meat cutter Nikolai relaxes after a meal in his West Coast home — as his wife was off meeting with a Soviet spy official.

43

who had been arrested at Disneyland. She delivered a suitcase from vice consul Gennady Prishchepa to a Los Angeles businessman. She once got a call from consul Yury Kurov about a possible mutiny among the crew of a Russian freighter docked in San Pedro, so she drove down there, told the captain she was from the Consulate in San Francisco, and held things in order until help could arrive. She even flew to Washington, D.C., visited the Soviet Embassy, and had a long chat with a high KGB officer about her work.

Nikolai says he knew little or nothing about all this, just that her behavior was getting odder and odder. "One night, when I came home from work, I found Svetlana looking very pretty; she was dressed up for a night on the town," he recalls. "To my great surprise, there was also a delicious dinner ready, with a bottle of wine. 'Did you have some good news today?' I asked. 'Don't rush things; let's eat first and talk later,' she told me. After dinner, we sat on the sofa. 'Now,' she said, 'I think congratulations are in order. I had a call today from San Francisco, from Mr. Chikvaidze himself, who said there were two films coming our way from Moscow very soon. So tomorrow we should begin to look at theaters to rent and think about advertising.'

"I was instantly alert. 'And what do they want in return, these dear friends of yours?' I asked. At first she tried to insist they wanted nothing. Then, after a long argument, she admitted there was one little job to be done. A package of papers had to be delivered to an address in San Francisco — to a man in a restaurant. For complicated reasons, she couldn't go herself, because she had to be somewhere else. Would I please make this one trip for her, to prove I was worthy of their friendship? I cursed her for being a fool and walked out into the night.

"As I walked, I began to think and ask myself questions. Should I leave her? Should I call the FBI and tell them what I knew? Would anyone believe even now that I wasn't involved? And then, after I'd been walking a long time, I thought, maybe it wasn't so bad. All I had to do was make one little trip and hand over some papers. . . .

"I found Svetlana sitting up in an armchair, her eyes closed, waiting for me. 'I'll do what you ask, on one condition,' I said quickly. 'That you'll drop this silly nonsense once and for all.' Svetlana burst into tears. 'I swear on our son that this will be the end of it!' she said. For some reason, I wanted to believe her.

"And so it was that I flew to San Francisco, met some guy in a café, gave him a package in silence, and went on my way. On the flight up, I had opened the envelope and looked at the papers, which seemed to be about FBI investigations into the characters of some Russians living in Los Angeles. Where Svetlana had gotten them and why the Soviet Consulate wanted them I didn't care or ask. I was glad to get back home, forget about the trip, and hope that things would improve. I wanted to believe that she had stopped, but I knew she really hadn't.

"The film business did help us a lot. After a while, both Svetlana and I had to fly back to Moscow to get the films. We did this by getting from an agency in Beverly Hills special visas which said that we weren't born in Russia. I went twice, and she went about six times. In the summer, our son went to Artek a couple of times, where he was accepted and treated very well. The money for the tickets used up what we made on showing the movies, but I was still working hard at the meat plant, earning overtime whenever I could, so we had enough money.

"At one point," Nikolai recalls, "we tried to make the movie business bigger by making a deal with an American company to distribute Russian films. Donald Levinson, a lawyer recommended by my boss, had helped us with a couple of lawsuits in the early days. Frankly, it was a thing we learned from other Russian immigrants, a way to make money. Now this Levinson set up some meetings for Svetlana with people from MGM and other companies, but nothing ever came of it. Our troubles with Levinson weren't over, however.

"But in spite of the extra money, our marriage was in bad shape, and getting worse. Svetlana was still coming home late, often very drunk, and when I asked where she had been it was always 'out with her friends' — Berta and a woman called Nina Thomas and others I never met. My threats and even hitting her occasionally didn't change her. I walked out once and stayed away three days, but I came back because I missed my son. He was the reason I stayed, and he was also the reason why I could never throw Svetlana out, no matter how badly she behaved. She was his mother; how could he ever forgive me if I did that? I did put in for separation papers in 1982, but we continued to live together in the same apartment.

"One night I had made supper for Matthew and myself and my nephew who was visiting from New York. It was 11 P.M. and Svetlana wasn't home. Suddenly, the phone rang: it was a friend of hers, Lena, who told me Svetlana got so drunk that she fell down and was lying unconscious on the sidewalk. What should she do, call an ambulance or the police? I told her I'd be right over. So in the middle of the night I picked my wife up off the street and brought her home. Of course in the morning she didn't remember anything.

"Another time, it was 10 P.M. and I was working late, Matthew was sleeping on the sofa, when Svetlana rushed in, drunk out of her mind, grabbed my Colt pistol which I had a permit for and always kept in the night table drawer, and started cursing him and throwing dishes around. 'I'll kill you, you little bastard!' she was shouting at the boy. 'You and your rotten father both!' Matthew ran crying to our neighbors' door, and luckily they were there to let him. When I got back, at about midnight, Svetlana had passed out on the living room floor, my gun next to her."

"All this time, of course, Svetlana was continuing to see the FBI agent John Hunt — giving him small presents, a watch and a shirt, telling him about what other Russian immigrants were doing, who knows what else? But from hints she dropped and things I overheard her say on the telephone, I suspected that things were not going well between her and Mr. Hunt. That's why in May of 1984 she set up a meeting at the FBI office with Richard Miller. I think she had heard about Miller from Hunt — that Miller was in trouble at the office, that he always needed money. Anyway, later that evening, she mentioned casually, 'Oh, by the way, I met another FBI man today. I'll introduce you to him, if you like.' I told her that I had no interest in meeting any more of her troublemaking friends, Russians or Americans. I thought that was the end of it, but one night later in the summer, she came home very late and very drunk, and said there was someone downstairs that I had to meet. She dragged me down to the street where I saw this very large person in a wrinkled suit, stomach sticking out through his shirt. He stuck out his hand, so I shook it. Then we talk a short walk down the block. He was muttering in English, I was muttering in Russian — to tell the truth, neither of us knew what the other was talking about it. It was only later, after the arrests, that I realized this man was Richard Miller."

Chapter 4

LOOKING FOR LEVCHENKO

*High-ranking Soviet-KGB
defector Stanislav Levchenko*

BUT before the episode with Richard Miller could begin, another and even stranger adventure was in store for Svetlana and Nikolai. It was during one of her trips to Moscow, supposedly in search of films in October of 1983, that Svetlana had a meeting with a high-level KGB officer. At this meeting, she was quizzed by the Russian about her relationship with FBI agent John Hunt, and then she was encouraged to meet other FBI agents and make use of their friendship. And just before she left, the KGB officer asked if she had ever heard the name Stanislav Levchenko.

"Levchenko? Of course. Who hasn't heard about the highest-ranking KGB man ever to defect to the West?" Svetlana later told Nikolai she had replied. "Why are you asking about him?"

"Because we have reason to believe that the traitor Levchenko is hiding out in California. We want him back home very badly, as you can imagine, and are willing to pay a lot of money to the person who helps us make that happen. Are you interested?"

"Of course I'm interested," Svetlana told him. "But I don't see what I can do."

52

"One thing you can do is casually mention his name among your FBI friends and see how they react," the KGB man said. "And you can also do some digging around on your own. Use your initiative! You're an attractive and clever woman; do what has to be done!"

Major Stanislav Levchenko had by 1983 become the KGB's, and the Soviet Union's, single largest embarrassment. A brilliant and handsome man, Levchenko was born in 1941, the son of a leading research scientist. Stanislav was just twenty-seven when transferred from GRU (Military Intelligence) to the KGB and proceeded to move rapidly up the ladder. In 1973 he landed a plum job — as Tokyo correspondent for the magazine *New Times*, which was really a cover for his work as one of the KGB's most important agents inside Japan. That country had become an important psychological battleground between Russia and the United States on one hand, and between Russia and China on the other. Levchenko's hero and role model was Richard Sorge, the famous Russian agent who worked in Japan before and during World War II. But almost as soon as he arrived in Japan and began working as a spy, Levchenko's disillusionment with the Soviet system began.

Levchenko worked with Japanese journalists, politicians, and businessmen, supplying them with money and favors in return for information about the Japanese system and influence that could be useful to Russia. He had advance knowledge of the Lockheed bribery scandal that shook the Japanese government, but Moscow doubted his sources and refused to let him use the information. To stir up trouble in China, he arranged for the Japanese publication of a fake will supposedly written by the late Chinese leader Zhou Enlai, but actually

53

forged by the KGB. Once he even found a source inside Japanese intelligence who provided him with reports on the surveillance by Japanese counterintelligence of known or suspected KGB agents. He got to see a copy of his own file, which labeled him as a "possible" KGB agent because his predecessor at the magazine had been an agent, but listed no other damaging evidence.

In spite of his good work in Tokyo, Levchenko had made enemies back in Moscow. One of them, a high KGB official, did everything in his power to deny Levchenko the credit and promotion he thought he deserved. But even this didn't bother him nearly as much as the cynical, cavalier attitude that his KGB superiors seemed to have toward their work and their country. Levchenko, who had become a secret Christian and attended church services whenever he could, was an idealist; he wanted desperately to believe he was on the right side and that what he was doing made some sense. His first trip home, in 1978, made him realize how much worse conditions were in Russia than in Japan. He also saw that the Soviet government was lying to the Russian people in the same way it lied to the Japanese, the Americans, and the Chinese. Back in Japan, he began to think seriously about defection.

On October 25, 1978, as he later described the scene to writer John Barron, Levchenko dressed casually in beige slacks, brown tweed sports jacket, and white shirt open at the collar. He forced down some breakfast, not sure when or where his next meal would be. Then he left his Tokyo apartment, stopped at a few of his regular places to keep any watchers off guard, and wound up outside the Hotel Sanno, near the U.S. Embassy, where he knew a reception was going on. He looked over the party guests and carefully chose a man wearing the uniform of a commander in the U.S. Navy, knowing that naval officers are trained to make quick decisions. "My name is Stanislav Levchenko, and I'm the Tokyo correspondent for the Soviet magazine *New Times*," he told the commander. "I urgently need to talk to a responsible American intelligence officer."

"Why an intelligence officer?" the commander asked.

"Because I have very sensitive business to discuss," Levchenko answered. After thinking for a moment, the commander led Levchenko to an empty room, placed two military sentries on duty outside, and said he would be back with someone within thirty minutes. True to his word, he returned with a tall, gray-haired, aristocratic-looking man who introduced himself as "Robert" and showed him some official identification. "Thank you," Levchenko told him with relief. "I'm a major in the KGB, and I request political asylum in the United States."

When the stunned "Robert" had convinced himself with a few questions that Levchenko was genuine, he left and returned in twenty minutes with another senior American official. "The United States grants you political asylum," they told him. "You can leave for America immediately. How's that for service?"

Levchenko told them he appreciated their efficiency, but now he was beginning to worry. If the KGB realized he was defecting, they would put as much pressure as they could on the Japanese not to let him leave the country. There was no way to predict what the touchy Japanese would do. The Americans hid Levchenko's car and took him to a safe house, while they made plans to fly him from Atsugi by military aircraft. For twelve hours Levchenko waited, tried to sleep, and worried about all the ways he knew that the KGB could kill him if he fell into their hands for even a few minutes. He had heard of an invisible powder, which you rubbed on your hand just before you met your victim. After you shook hands, you had five minutes to apply an antidote. Seven or eight days later, the person you touched died of cardiac arrest.

For some reason, Washington rejected the idea of a military plane; they would have to travel on a commercial airline. Levchenko predicted trouble at the airport, and sure enough he was spotted by Japanese counterintelligence and questioned. For five hours, as flight after flight left for America, Levchenko calmly held the Japanese at bay and refused to talk to any Soviet officials. Finally, just as a carload of KGB heavies arrived at the airport, United States pressure on the Japanese Foreign Office paid off. Levchenko was told he was free to go and put aboard a Pan American flight to Los Angeles. The next day he was at CIA headquarters in Langley, Virginia, beginning his long debriefing on the secret world of the KGB.

So it wasn't surprising that Levchenko should have become such a prime target for Soviet intelligence, or that they would stoop to using even low-level sources like Svetlana Ogorodnikova in their desperate attempts to bring him back to justice in Russia. In spite of an announcement to the world that Levchenko had been caught, tried, and executed in 1981, everybody knew he was really alive and in hiding in the United States.

The day after the Ogorodnikovs and Miller were arrested, lawyer Donald E. Levinson — who had filed some personal injury suits for Nikolai and Svetlana, and who had also set up a few meetings with potential film distributors — called the FBI and said he had some information that might prove useful in the case. The next day, Levinson was interviewed by FBI agents and told them a fantastic story. He said that Nikolai had called him over to his apartment and, while they were walking around the block, asked for his help in locating a Russian named Stanislav Levchenko, who was probably living somewhere in California under an assumed name. It seemed that this Levchenko impregnated a friend of the Ogorodnikovs, and now the woman wanted to find her child's father and file a paternity suit. Nikolai told Levinson that the woman had plenty of money, paid him a cash advance of $200 and another $500 later on for his services, and said there would be a further payment of $10,000 when and if he found Levchenko. Later, at the Ogorodnikovs' apartment, Levinson said that Nikolai loaned him a book called *KGB Today: The Hidden Hand*, by John Barron, which contained several chapters about Levchenko. (Nikolai, who denies all involvement in the Levchenko affair, says the book wasn't his, he doesn't read English well enough to read books in that language, and that if anyone gave the book to Levinson it was Svetlana.)

Levinson, whose father owned the meat-packing plant where Nikolai worked, also told the FBI about a dinner he had attended one evening in 1982 at Mischa's. On hand were Nikolai and Svetlana, two Russians from the San Francisco Consulate — later identified as Gennady Prishchepa and Boris Belyakov — and their wives, plus an unidentified older woman who Levinson said "looked like a football player" and who never said anything. The dinner was part of Levinson's plan to sign an American film company as the official distributor for old Russian movies. "But the Soviets always insisted on money up front, so the deal fell apart," Levinson told the FBI. In addition, his statement to the FBI included observations about the Ogorodnikovs' life-style ("They lived like pigs but always had money) and Svetlana's intelligence (Levinson found her "deceptively brilliant)."

Levinson never seems to have done anything to locate Levchenko or earn his $700 advance other than attempt to run a Department of Motor Vehicles check. Nikolai says the advance was movie deal money, which he tried in vain to get back. ("Every time I call him, there's a different number, or no number, or a new address," he recalls.) But there is some evidence that Svetlana also recruited another acquaintance, a young Russian immigrant living in Los Angeles who had a criminal background, into the KGB hunt for the missing defector. This young man, known as Vadim, reportedly went to the Hotel Bristol in Warsaw, Poland, in September of 1983, where he was briefed by the KGB and given a cash advance. In November of that year, San Francisco newspapers carried a small story about a Russian businessman, Ivan Levchuk, who was severely beaten after a robbery. Levchuk, it turned out, really was Levchuk — not Levchenko, as Vadim had been tipped. Vadim and Svetlana, who had recommended him in the first place, were chastised by Grishin and Chikvaidze. It seems that the pinnacle of her career as a spy had yet to be reached.

THE 250-POUND TIME BOMB

College year book captions don't tell the complete story. The caption to this snap shot of Richard Miller in the Brigham Young University Yearbook did not suggest that one day he would spy for the Soviet Union.

"**T**HE day that Svetlana met Richard Miller was the worst day of our lives," says Nikolai now. But May 24, 1984, didn't seem particularly bleak or momentous at the time. Svetlana had definitely worn out her welcome with John Hunt; the FBI man was getting ready to retire and didn't want to have anything more to do with her. But her friends in San Francisco continued to press her for more information, more contacts. So on May 24 she placed a call to the FBI office in the Federal Building in Westwood and asked to talk to Richard Miller. She told him she had been recommended by a mutual friend, "David," and could supply information about the Russian immigrant community in Los Angeles, if he was interested. Miller wasn't very enthusiastic, but things were slow in his department so he set up an appointment for the next day.

Either Svetlana wasn't looking her best (she could appear glamorous if she made an effort but often seemed drab and ordinary) or else Miller's libido was low that day, because no sparks flew between them. Miller later said he doubted that her information would be worth anything. Still, he didn't close the door

62

completely. They agreed to meet again the next day, and on the beach at Malibu they had sex for the first time. Two or three more dates followed; all involving meals and talk and sex. By this time Miller was beginning to see her as a way out of his massive work problems.

By early August, when Svetlana called again after a trip to Russia, Miller had had the chance to check her name in the FBI's informant files, and to listen to a lecture from John Hunt about not getting involved too closely with her. He had also been on the receiving end of another warning about his weight from his FBI superiors — who told him, in effect, "Shape up or ship out." For Miller, whose idea of a pleasant lunch hour was eating candy bars and reading comic books in a local convenience store just down Wilshire Boulevard from his office, shaping up wasn't that easy. Also, things at home weren't going as well as they might be. His affair with a married Mormon woman had been discovered by her husband, and had caused them both to be kicked out of the Church. Money was short, and the avacado-growing business he'd gone into with his father-in-law was costing more than it brought in. In effect, Richard Miller by this time was a 250-pound time bomb waiting to go off — and Svetlana Ogorodnikova was the fuse.

The meals and sex resumed, in Long Beach and Monterey Park and Malibu. Over dinner at the Chart House in Malibu, as they enjoyed their shrimp cocktails and swordfish steaks and California chablis, Richard began to pour out his troubles to this very sympathetic woman. Over coffee, she dropped her first bombshell. She wasn't just a pretty face, Svetlana told him; she was a major in the KGB (just like Levchenko — perhaps this was where she got the idea) and was authorized to pay

Photo: Anatole Verbitzky

Photo: Anatole Verbitzky

Freed from their harsh life in the Soviet Union, the Ogorodnikov's enjoy the comforts of life in California: (below) Nikolai toasts friends; (bottom, left) the Ogorodnikov's throw a surprise birthday party for son, Matthew, and (top, left) Svetlana decorates a Christmas tree.
(During this time, she was also seducing an FBI agent into spying for the U.S.S.R.!)

Photo: Anatole Verbizky

65

lots of money for useful documents. Perhaps they could help each other: he giving her documents that would keep her bosses in San Francisco happy, she giving him the cash he needed.

It was at this meeting, or perhaps one the next night, that Miller told Svetlana he wouldn't consider doing anything like that — and if he did, it would have to be for nothing less than one or two million dollars. Three days later, again at dinner, she asked him if he would like to meet with someone that night and talk about money. Miller agreed, and Svetlana went off to make a phone call. "It's all arranged; we're meeting him later," she said — and then proceeded to get very drunk.

At about 1 A.M., following her mumbled instructions, Miller drove east in his Isuzu to 1155 North Gardner Street in Hollywood. Svetlana took him upstairs to her apartment, where he met a man he later described as being "about sixty years old" who introduced himself as Nikolai Wolfson. Svetlana said that this Wolfson had thirty years of experience in handling financial affairs for the "network" and was authorized to pay Miller for his help. Miller and Wolfson walked downstairs into the basement garage of the apartment building, where, Miller says, they talked about the details of supplying FBI documents to Svetlana. It would have to be in Mexico, Miller said; Wolfson said that would be no problem. Miller, his dreams of a million dollars abandoned to reality, said he would need an initial payment of $50,000 in gold, to be stored in three safety deposit boxes; Wolfson said that would be no problem. Miller also asked for $15,000 in cash, $7,000 of which Svetlana would carry back across the border for him to avoid currency restrictions. Again, Wolfson assured him this would be no problem. Miller gave him his FBI business card, and they shook hands and parted. Wolfson went back upstairs, and Miller drove to the FBI office in Westwood.

At 2 A.M., Miller ran a check on Nikolai Wolfson. He turned out to be listed in the files of Russian immigrants as Nikolai Ogorodnikov, Svetlana's husband, who had filed for separation in 1982 but continued to live at the Gardner Street address. Whether this information had any effect on Miller's plans or thoughts at this point is hard to tell. If he thought he was going to make money selling documents to the Russians, wouldn't the fact that Wolfson was really a $400-a-week meat cutter have raised some serious doubts in his mind? On the other hand, if he had already thought about trying to penetrate a major Russian spy ring, wouldn't this obvious lie have made him aware that he was dealing with amateurs?

Whatever his thoughts, Miller kept them to himself. But about this time, he did one of the few smart things that seemed to indicate he knew the kind of trouble he could be getting into. He contacted a private detective in Riverside — Larry Grayson — the same man he used to earn a few extra dollars from by supplying him with information. He asked if Grayson could arrange to have him photographed secretly at an upcoming meeting in Mexico. Grayson said it could be done, for a few hundred dollars, but Miller never followed up on his impulse to cover his tail.

He and Svetlana continued to meet, have sex and dinner, and make plans. She told him that she had to deliver some film canisters to the Soviet Consulate in San Francisco on August 24; why couldn't they both drive up and have some fun along the way? And since they were going anyway, could he come up with some little FBI document so that she could show her friends that he was serious about doing business with them? Miller agreed, and at some point in the next few days he took from the files and copied on a machine in his office a twenty-four-page FBI document entitled *Reporting Guidance: Foreign Intelligence Information*, dated March 15, 1983. The document was stamped "SECRET" in red on the original, which was found later in Miller's Lynwood house.

He handed her the copy as they left for San Francisco, in her car, on the morning of August 24. They spent the night in a motel in Lost Hills, outside of Bakersfield, then proceeded on to San Francisco, arriving about lunchtime. "I need something to take inside to prove to them that you're a real FBI man," Svetlana said as they got near the Soviet Consulate on Green Street. Miller handed over his black leather pass case containing his FBI shield and his official ID card. She dropped him in front of a restaurant on Union Street, saying she'd be back soon. Then she drove off with her film canisters. Inside one was the copy of the report that Miller had made.

Three hours later, Svetlana was back, returning Miller's pass case and saying everybody was pleased. After a pleasant night in a motel in Livermore, on the Oakland side of San Francisco Bay, the couple headed back to Los Angeles on August 26. During the journey back, Svetlana told Richard that they had been followed and photographed by the KGB for the last day and a half. This news didn't cause Miller any problems; presumably he wasn't concerned that he, a trained FBI agent, didn't notice any of the surveillance.

That particular visit to the Soviet Consulate was probably the one that set the FBI's own surveillance machinery in motion. They spotted Svetlana's car, checked the plates to her Hollywood address, and on September 1 began tapping her phone and watching her activities. So many men in business suits, driving clean new cars, began showing up in the neighborhood that even their son Matthew commented on it and began to worry about what might be happening.

"One night in early September, I came home from work, made supper for Matthew, and then fell asleep in my chair," Nikolai recalls. "I woke up to find somebody pulling on my sleeve. 'Dad, wake up! Why don't you turn on the lamp? Why are you sitting here in the dark?' It turned out that Matthew wanted me to help translate something from Russian into English. 'Why don't you ask your mother?' I said. 'Her English is better than mine.'

" 'How can I?' my boy answered. 'When she comes home, I'm already asleep. Dad, what's happening? Why are you always so sad, and why is Mother always so angry? I know she doesn't like living in this strange country, but is that what's bothering you, too?'

" 'My dear son,' I answered him, 'how can I tell you about it? You're very smart and sensitive, but you wouldn't understand it all. No, I don't miss Kiev — living here isn't bad. I'm troubled by something else. But to tell you the truth, we'd all be better off if we'd never left Russia.'

69

"We sat there, my son and I, talking and hugging each other, until Svetlana came in, about midnight, looking worried and sick. She immediately began to shout at the boy for being up so late. When Matthew had gone off to bed, she turned on me. I tried to calm her down, telling her she was behaving like a crazy person. 'You're playing a very dangerous game, Svetlana,' I warned her. 'You are still seeing Grishin, seeing Miller; between them, they'll both pull you under.'

" 'If I go down, so will you!' she screamed back at me. 'I've at least got an excuse. I'm sick. If I get caught, I'll plead insanity. I'm a mentally unstable person, so what can they expect of me? I'll tell them the story of having an affair with Andropov that should make their hair stand on end! And you, Mr. Meat Cutter, Mr. Big Time Kiever, Mr. Jew — what will you say when the axe falls, you squealer?'

"I told her that I had thought about that many times, and I hoped they would believe me when I told the truth — that I did what I felt I had to do to protect my son. 'But as for you, aren't you worried?' I asked. 'Haven't you heard that America is bringing back the death penalty for spies?'

"Svetlana tried to laugh, but instead she turned even more pale and rushed off into her bedroom. For the next hour, I heard her tearing up papers and flushing them down the toilet."

In spite of any fears, Svetlana knew she was in deep and there was no way to get out. She had promised to deliver Miller to a meeting outside the country, and now she had to pull it off. On Tuesday evening, September 11, Grishin called her, and the FBI listened as they talked in Russian about making arrangements to bring her "friend" over. Exactly a week later, on September 18, Grishin called again — at almost the exact time, 7:45 P.M. Svetlana told him that her friend had agreed "in principle" to a trip but wanted it to be to Mexico. Grishin insisted on Europe — Warsaw or Vienna. Svetlana agreed and said she would persuade her friend. "And make sure he brings all his baggage with him," said Grishin. "I mean, that will help him on vacation."

That call ended at 8 P.M. Three minutes later, an FBI surveillance team saw Svetlana and Nikolai leave their apartment and walk around the neighboring streets for two hours. "It was the usual argument," Nikolai remembers. "She said she had to go to Vienna, and I had to help her make the arrangements. We left the apartment because I didn't want to upset Matthew with our fighting."

The time bomb was ticking faster now. On September 20, Miller called Svetlana at home, making final arrangements to meet her that evening at 6 P.M. "at the Casino." Svetlana was observed by the FBI as she left her apartment at 5:04, drove slowly around the block to the west, then slowly around the block to the east. She then parked on the south side of Vista Street for several minutes, before turning west on Santa Monica Boulevard. She stopped and entered a liquor store, then circled one block north and one block south before continuing west on Santa Monica Boulevard. "Either she hated making left turns or she thought she could shake off anybody following her," one FBI agent later commented.

At 6:11 P.M., delayed by rush-hour traffic, Svetlana joined Miller at the Café Casino in Santa Monica. They were both nervous and ducked out a side door without eating. An FBI surveillance team tracked them as they drove down toward Marina del Rey in her car, pulled into a McDonald's for take-out drinks, then drove back to Santa Monica where they checked into a motel and stayed for two hours before returning to the Café Casino to pick up his car. Svetlana got home at about 10:52 — traffic was light at that hour — and at 10:56 she and Nikolai were seen taking another nightime stroll, this one lasting thirty minutes.

Miller called Svetlana the next day. She said, "Don't forget our date on Wednesday." He assured her that he wouldn't, then said that he'd gone downstairs that morning "and got an application for that item." Miller's application for a passport was filed on September 21, 1984, at the U.S. Passport Service office in the Federal Building. It listed Mexico as his intended destination, "translator" as his occupation, and October 10, 1984, as his intended date of departure. The fact that Americans, especially Californians, don't need a passport to visit Mexico indicates that Miller must have been keeping his European options open. He closed the conversation by repeating that he would see Svetlana on Wednesday.

That was Friday. On Monday, September 24, FBI agents in San Francisco watched Nikolai arrive on an 8:15 A.M. PSA flight from Los Angeles, carrying a gray film canister. He caught a bus at the airport and got off in downtown San Francisco. From there, they watched him follow a strange route to the Soviet Consulate on Green Street. He would talk to someone on the street, take a bus, get off, talk to someone else, then take another bus, finally arriving at the Consulate at 10:20. Nikolai insists that what looked to the FBI like an attempt to avoid surveillance was really caused by his forgetting how to get to the Consulate and having to ask directions often.

Nikolai stayed in the Consulate just fifteen minutes and came out without the film canister. Then he was seen to go back inside, stay another fifteen minutes, and come out carrying what the FBI said was "a green book." He walked for a while, then entered a Bank of America branch on Union Street where the FBI says he received a "large wad" of bills from a teller. Nikolai says he needed money for the bus to the airport, withdrew $20 from his own account, and got the money in fives and ones. A withdrawal slip dated September 24, 1986, from that branch, in the amount of $20, was found in the Ogorodnikovs' apartment when they were arrested.

On Tuesday, September 25, Svetlana called travel agent Diana Baskevitch of Beverly International Travel, with whom she had done business before. "How are my tickets coming?" Svetlana asked. Baskevitch said she and her companion would be taking Capitol Air from Los Angeles to Frankfurt, West Germany, and then a Lufthansa flight to Vienna. Svetlana told Baskevitch that the departure date would definitely be October 10 — "that's the only time he can go."

That night, Grishin made his regular weekly call, at 7:26 P.M. He asked about travel arrangements for the upcoming "vacation," and Svetlana assured him that they would arrive at 11:40 on the morning of October 11.

The next day was Wednesday, September 26, and Miller and Svetlana had a date to go shopping for clothes. Their FBI tails saw them go into several men's stores, looking at suits and finally putting a hold on the very expensive Burberry trench coat that was later seized as evidence. During that outing, they discussed final details of the trip. Miller said he would be picking up his passport the next day; she told him how they'd be flying to Vienna, and then described the route back: a Jordanian Airlines flight to Geneva, and then a TWA flight to New York and Los Angeles, getting back on October 14. The tickets would cost $4,000, she said; their friends in San Francisco were picking up the tab. And she revealed for the first time that they would be meeting with a man called "Mikhail," a general not in the KGB but in its rival GRU, Russian Military Intelligence.

Maybe it was this last news that made Miller began to worry, or maybe he did notice the FBI surveillance car parked forty feet away in the Little League parking lot near his office building the day before, as the prosecution would later claim. Anyway, he drove back to Lynwood that night, ate some take-out Chinese food, paced up and down, tried to sleep but couldn't. Sometime in the early hours of the morning, he said, he came to a decision. His plan — to go with Svetlana to Vienna and convince the Russians that he really was ready to work for them — was too big, too ambitious, too dangerous for one man to pull off. He had to tell his superiors everything, and risk their anger at him for having gone so far on his own.

The time bomb finally exploded. Miller walked into the office of his immediate superior, P. Bryce Christensen, about 11 A.M. on September 27, and told him he wanted to make a statement. "I've been trying to infiltrate the KGB," he said, and his words made Christensen's jaw drop. For almost a month, Christensen and his chief, Richard T. Bretzing, had been reading transcripts of all the wiretap evidence building against Miller, and had been listening to reports from agents who had been following, photographing, and videotaping Miller and Svetlana. On the basis of what was developing, the U.S. Justice Department's top expert on espionage — John Martin, head of the internal security division — had flown in from Washington specifically to handle the case. Now Miller was standing in front of Christensen and saying he was trying to infiltrate the KGB? Was he even dumber than he looked and acted — or a lot smarter?

When he heard about Miller's statement, Martin snorted, "You guys don't have a prosecutable case," as he packed his bag and headed back for Washington. The FBI had no direct evidence that Miller had actually passed any documents to the Russians, and if he stuck to his story there wouldn't be any way for the FBI to make espionage charges hold up in court.

But Christensen had another idea. Why not grill Miller for a few days — test his story to see how well it held up? They might be able to salvage enough to justify all the expense of their investigation so far. At the very least, they should collect enough to let them finally fire Miller's fat ass right out of the FBI.

The first days of Miller's examination by fellow FBI agents didn't turn up much, just names and dates and details of sexual encounters, most of which they already knew about anyway. At this point, the interrogators were almost sure that Miller would beat the espionage rap. He'd be fired, for sure, because of his relationship with Svetlana, but there was just not enough hard evidence for an indictment or a court case. Then, on September 29, Bretzing talked to Miller, took him through what Mormons call "the five steps of the process." At the end of it, Miller agreed to take a polygraph test. When he failed that, he finally started to give his interrogators what they needed — dates and details of passing to Svetlana the twenty-four-page FBI booklet which she later dropped off at the Soviet Consulate. He also gave them permission to search his Lynwood house, where the original of that booklet and other classified FBI documents were found scattered around the untidy, partially-furnished premises.

While Miller was spilling his guts in Westwood, a few miles east in Hollywood the panic had begun. Svetlana had been expecting to hear from Miller that he had picked up his passport and had arranged to be away from home and office from October 10 through 14. On September 28, she called him — first at his office, where she was told he was "out," and then, between 4 P.M. and 11:37 P.M., fifteen times at his Lynwood number. That night, there was little sleep in the Gardner Street apartment. Nikolai remembers Svetlana pacing up and down, watching the phone. "I asked her what was going on, but she told me to mind my own damned business," he recalls. "I knew she was planning some trip, she had mentioned it already and had given me instructions about looking after Matthew, but I didn't know when it was supposed to happen."

Svetlana tried Miller again at Lynwood several times the next day, and the two days after that. She decided finally that he had gone down to Bonsall to be with his family, and that he would call when he got back. He was in tact back home in Bonsall, driven there by Bryce Christensen on October 1, but there would be no more calls to Svetlana.

On Tuesday, October 2, the FBI decided it had collected enough evidence to charge Miller and Svetlana with espionage. The evidence against Nikolai was definitely less solid, but they decided to take him as well. Warrants for the Ogorodnikovs were issued at 10 P.M. that night.

Miller was arrested in the afternoon of October 2 at his home in Bonsall. He was fired from the FBI and charged with espionage and related crimes. At about midnight, while Nikolai was sleeping on a sofa in his living room, with Matthew on another sofa and a young cousin of Nikolai's visiting from New York in a bedroll on the floor, he was awakened by noises on the landing outside his kitchen window. "I grabbed my gun from the end table where I always kept it and walked toward the kitchen," Nikolai recalls. "I thought it was robbers; maybe if they saw my gun they would be scared and go away. Instead I heard voices — 'Nikolai! Nikolai! It's the FBI! Put down the gun!' So I threw it quickly down and opened the door." According to FBI officials, Nikolai was "very lucky" that he wasn't shot.

As several of the agents hustled Nikolai and Svetlana off to jail, others stayed behind to execute the search warrant that Bryce Christensen had applied for. Among the items collected were two human teeth; a wooden clipper ship; Nikolai's latest paycheck, for $314.13, and his AAA card; three exit visas from Russia for Israel, dated January 23, 1973; food stamps and Medi-Cal cards in the names of Svetlana and Matthew Ogorodnikov; a piece of paper with the number of the Soviet Consulate in San Francisco written on it — (415) 567-3083; a bank check-cashing card in Svetlana's name; and a receipt for a Motel 6 in Hayward, California, in the amount of $28.50, dated July 25, 1984. It all added up to the wreckage of three lives.

Chapter 6

CAUGHT IN THE MACHINE

SVETLANA and Nikolai were taken, in different cars, to the FBI office in Westwood for interrogation. His biggest worry, he recalls, was about his son. "I only had a second to tell Matthew that we were being arrested, that we hadn't done anything, that we'd be home soon," Nikolai says. "I told him to be a good boy and do what my cousin John tells him. He started to cry, but they took us away fast so I couldn't say more." After five hours of questioning, Nikolai went to the Federal prison at Terminal Island, where Richard Miller was also a guest. Svetlana was taken to Sybil Brand Institute, the women's prison in downtown Los Angeles. Then the gears of the legal machine began to grind. Because he had no money for a private lawyer, the Federal Public Defender's office appointed Randy Sue Pollock to look after Nikolai's interests.

"At our first meeting the next day, after about an hour of talk, my investigator casually asked him, 'How long have you been a Russian spy?'" recalls Pollock, now in private practice in the San Francisco area. "Nikolai's reaction was very natural and believable — he gave a surprised laugh and answered, 'What? I'm not!' "

The case was assigned to U.S. District Court Judge David V. Kenyon, who had a reputation for being tough but fair. One of the first things he did was to issue an order restraining attorneys on both sides from talking to the press. Svetlana got a pair of young lawyers from the prestigious Los Angeles law firm of Munger, Tolles and Rickleshaus — Brad D. Brian and Gregory Stone, who were picked from the Federal Indigent Panel. Miller's family at first tried to hire the team of Howard Weitzman and Donald Re, who had just helped John DeLorean beat his Federal drug rap. But Weitzman and Re, who still hadn't collected most of the money DeLorean owed them, eventually declined, and two former U.S. prosecutors, Stanley L. Greenberg and Joel Levine, took over Miller's defense. Levine was no stranger to big espionage trials; he was co-prosecutor in the famous "Falcon and the Snowman" case.

On Friday, October 13, a Federal grand jury handed down a thirteen-count indictment against Richard W. Miller and Nikolai and Svetlana Ogorodnikov, charging them with espionage, bribery, and the unlawful delivery and receipt of classified documents. Each of them could receive a life sentence on each charge if convicted; all three subsequently entered not guilty pleas to the charges. Also named as an unindicted co-conspirator was Aleksandr Grishin, vice consul at the Soviet Consulate in San Francisco. Because of his diplomatic immunity, Grishin couldn't be prosecuted; he denied all the charges, said he had never heard of Miller and the Ogorodnikovs, and was soon transferred back to Moscow. Later, Bruce G. Merritt, who as Assistant U.S. Attorney headed the team that prosecuted Nikolai and Svetlana, would tell the press that Miller had been offered a twenty-five-year sentence if he pleaded guilty.

"At the indictment stage, the hope was that somebody would plead; that Miller would see the light, plead guilty, and then testify against the Ogorodnikovs," Merritt said. "We talked plea with Miller, but he wouldn't have it. His lawyers weren't that interested." Merritt said that the case against Miller was viewed as the strongest of the three, because he had admitted to seven different FBI agents that he had passed documents to Svetlana. He added that prosecutors shared the view of defense lawyers that the weakest Government case was the one against Nikolai. "Had it not been for all the walks that Nikolai took with Svetlana, we probably wouldn't have arrested him at all," said Merritt. "We thought he was at least as deeply involved as Svetlana, but the case against him was thin."

Miller's story about his attempts to use Svetlana to save his job by penetrating a Soviet spy ring first hit the press on October 16, the same day that internal investigators from FBI headquarters in Washington arrived in Los Angeles to look into the Miller affair. It would be the first, but definitely not the last, time that the Bureau found itself denying charges of Mormon favoritism. A month after the original indictment, the Government filed a second list of felony charges against Miller — accusing him of skimming off money he was supposed to pay to informants and of selling biographical information from FBI files to Riverside private detective Larry Grayson.

Stanley Greenberg said the new charges were "a reflection of how weak the Government's case is. A few weeks ago they accused this guy of selling out his country, one of the worst things you can accuse someone of. Now they're accusing him of stealing paper clips out of the supply closet."

On December 12, with a tentative trial date of February 12, 1985, set for all three defendants, Svetlana's lawyers filed an affidavit saying she was never told of her rights on the night she was arrested (a few days before, the wife of a Czech spy caught in New York was released when she made similar charges), and that FBI agents threatened to tell Nikolai of her affair with Miller if she didn't confess. Svetlana's drinking habits and mental problems were first made public at a pretrial hearing shortly thereafter, when Judge Kenyon ordered the prosecution to turn over to the defense all information it had relating to her mental stability. Prosecutor Merritt told the court that Svetlana once claimed to have had an affair with Soviet Premier Yuri Andropov and that she "tended to tell wild stories when she had been drinking heavily."

As the weeks of pretrial hearings and motions and affidavits dragged into months, it became obvious to the Government that its original plan — to try Miller first and then use him as chief witness against the Ogorodnikovs — wasn't going to work. Miller and his lawyers refused to bend; they had rejected another plea bargain and were actively talking about his defense of using Svetlana to penetrate the KGB. So the prosecution reversed itself, decided to put Nikolai and Svetlana on trial first and give Miller limited immunity so that he could be called as a prosecution witness. This meant they were so sure they had squeezed everything out of him they needed to eventually convict him that they would agree that anything new he said during the Ogorodnikovs' trial couldn't be used against him.

Because Judge Kenyon was working on another case, it was agreed by all parties that the Ogorodnikov trial would be a part-time affair — half-day sessions three or four days a week.

Assistant U.S. Attorney Richard B. Kendall, prosecuting the case with Merritt, began his opening statement on April 19, 1985. He told the jury that they would be hearing a case involving a conspiracy by the Russian KGB through the Ogorodnikovs to recruit FBI agent Richard Miller. He said that the Government would show how the KGB works inside the United States, using people like Nikolai and Svetlana, "who might best be described as utility agents," and would provide evidence of their work for the KGB from the time they arrived in this country in 1973 until Svetlana met Miller in May of 1984. Kendall then began to lay the foundation for expert testimony on how the KGB worked in America: operating out of diplomatic establishments like the Soviet Consulate in San Francisco, using residents who report directly to Moscow Center. "We will show that their primary objectives are to steal American science and technology, to influence American policies, and to penetrate the FBI," Kendall told the jury.

Because of the rule that restricts Soviet diplomats to within a twenty-five-mile radius of their Consulate, Kendall continued, the KGB has to use outside agents for much of its work. "The Ogorodnikovs were Soviet agents. They performed tasks for the KGB officers inside the Consulate. These agents are not necessarily trained. The Government is not going to contend that the Ogorodnikovs were trained agents. Because the Soviet Union has trouble finding agents in the United States, they will take just about anybody they can find," Kendall said. He then went on to talk about how the Government's expert witnesses would show the way that Aleksandr Grishin and Svetlana Ogorodnikova tried to "dry clean" themselves when they spoke, by using pay telephones and elaborate "plain language codes" to avoid surveillance.

"We will show how the Ogorodnikovs, as so-called Third Wave Russian immigrants, would normally not be allowed back to the Soviet Union as visitors," Kendall said. "Nevertheless, you'll see that between 1979 and 1984, members of the family made nine trips back and forth." The testimony of retired FBI agent John Hunt, Kendall continued, would show how Hunt had first become aware of Svetlana when she was tailed while driving Soviet vice consul Viktor Zonov around Los Angeles in 1980. At first she said she didn't want to cooperate with the FBI, but in February of 1982, after much vacillating, she agreed to become an FBI "asset" — someone who provides useful information. Hunt would tell how in June of that year she offered him a gift of a Russian doll outside a Hollywood nightclub called Simply Blues, threw her arms around him and said, "I love you. Let's go to a motel." Then, Kendall went on, the jury would see how Svetlana visited the KGB at the Soviet Embassy in Washington and told them she had a boyfriend in the FBI.

"Hunt established a nonsexual, professional relationship with Svetlana by introducing her to his wife, his daughter, and his grandchild, and by exchanging gifts with her," Kendall said. But Svetlana was too erratic; she kept on pushing for sex, so on January 27, 1983, he closed her asset file and stopped seeing her. She called him in March, saying she was dying of a rare blood disease. Hunt visited her with a doctor and found she was lying. With the KGB increasing their pressure on her to produce something from her FBI "boyfriend," Svetlana tried complaining about Hunt to his superiors. When that didn't work, she switched her attention to another FBI agent — Richard Miller. "We will show how Miller went against direct orders not to see Svetlana," Kendall said.

Hunt then mentioned Nikolai directly for the first time. After the sexual relationship between Miller and Svetlana began in May of 1984, he said, the Government would show how Nikolai started taking over some of Svetlana's KGB tasks, such as asking lawyer Donald Levinson to help find KGB defector Stanislav Levchenko. "Nikolai Ogorodnikov's overt involvement in the Miller scenario began no later than August 7th," Kendall added, referring to the night when he was introduced to Miller as Nikolai Wolfson. You will hear testimony from Richard Miller," Kendall said, "but you must remember that he is also charged in the case and what he says may well be self-serving. His testimony has to be received by you and judged by you very cautiously, with great care," he warned.

For the critical events of September of 1984, Kendall told the jury, the Government had prepared a chart of everyone's movements. Each major player had a special color code: purple was Svetlana, green was Nikolai, blue was Miller, red was Grishin. There would be symbols for cars, telephones, people walking. He gave a preview of the testimony they would hear about Svetlana's behavior on September 2, at Orbach's department store in Los Angeles, where she seemed to meet a balding man in his mid-fifties at the women's shoe table: "They communicated without looking at each other. Then he stuck his hand inside one particular shoe and took it out. She did the same. They parted silently. He disappeared into a nearby apartment building and has never been identified."

Kendall then played for the jury a tape of a telephone conversation in Russian between Svetlana and Grishin on September 11, with an English translation provided by subtitles on videotape. He tried to play an audiotape of a conversation between Miller and Svetlana in Miller's Isuzu, which had been bugged by the FBI on September 12. After some trouble about stereo equipment not picking up a mono tape, the jury finally heard Miller trying to start his car many times. "This is a great car, it just needs some work," Miller was heard to say. "After I get back from Mexico, I'll" — "You'll be able to sell this car and buy a new one," Svetlana interrupted. "The next sounds you hear will be of intimate behavior," Kendall told the jury apologetically. Then, Miller was heard to speak again: "You know what you've done? You've stolen my heart." Svetlana was heard to laugh, then say, "Well, I know this heart. It is my job."

After detailing the events of the visit to the Café Casino in Santa Monica on September 20, Kendall told the jury how they would hear about the shopping trip of September 26, with Miller and Svetlana trying to find a European-style suit for him but having to settle for the Burberry trench coat. Then he wound up his opening statement by bringing Nikolai back into the action. He told how Svetlana had instructed Grishin that if he called on October 9th and she was on her way to Vienna with Miller, "my husband will talk to you if I am gone."

Kendall concluded, "Nikolai Ogorodnikov played a smaller part in the conspiracy by following his wife's activities with Miller, by meeting with Miller, and by traveling to the Soviet Consulate on September 24 to get clarification for the trip to Vienna."

Svetlana's lawyer, Brad D. Brian, began his opening statement by reminding the jury that nothing that Kendall had just said to them was actual evidence. "We'll show that everything he has presented will prove instead that Svetlana was an FBI informer, long before she had ever met Mr. Miller," Brian told them. Characterizing Svetlana as a woman of "low intelligence," whose actions were "induced by the FBI," he said the defense would prove "that just as she was following Hunt's orders in 1982, so she was following Miller's orders in 1984. It wasn't illegal then, and it it's not illegal now."

Brian told the jury that the defense would show how Svetlana became depressed and alcoholic because of her relationship with Hunt. "And whatever Richard Miller says, the evidence will show that Svetlana thought she was helping the FBI. She was in effect a pawn, caught in the middle of a high-stakes chess game between Russian and American counterintelligence players," Brian said. Then, rapidly switching metaphors, he continued, "She was used by Hunt, and by Miller, as if she was a puppet with two strings — and the Russians were pulling the other string."

The defense would prove that the Ogorodnikovs' film business was totally legitimate, set up by a respected travel agency and not the Soviet Consulate, and that because of it "Svetlana had the chance to meet important people and go back to Russia." The calls to and from Aleksandr Grishin, he said, would be shown to be part of her going along with the FBI plan. And far from Svetlana being the dominant one, the defense "will prove that she was under Miller's control" during the entire operation. "The trial will be long," Brian said as he wrapped up his opening statement, "but we ask you to wait until you've heard all the evidence and the arguments. Don't make any judgments until the end."

Randy Sue Pollock tried hard to minimize Nikolai's role in her opening statement. "Despite how the prosecution described the evidence, what you will hear will not convince you that Mr. Ogorodnikov was in any way involved in the conspiracy to commit espionage," she told the jury. "Basically, what you will hear is about three other people — Svetlana, John Hunt, and Richard Miller." She went on to say that character witnesses would testify how hard Nikolai worked at his job as a meat cutter, how he had to be told by his boss not to come to work so early and that he should take a vacation. "You'll hear how much the film business meant to him; it was a connection with his homeland." It was true, she said, that Nikolai did miss Russia, and that he talked about it and criticized America at work and in Plummer Park. "But you will also come to know the personality of Russian émigrés, who are distrustful of authority. Nikolai Ogorodnikov took advantage of the privilege of living in America by speaking out loudly against some things, and the Russians who associated with him in Plummer Park could not understand how he could be so vocal."

As for all those long walks that the prosecution made so much of, Pollock told the jury that the defense would prove they were perfectly normal acts — the only times Nikolai and Svetlana could be alone, away from their son and Nikolai's cousin visiting from New York, to argue and talk about their problems.

The jury would see a videotape of how small their apartment was, and witnesses would testify how warm the evenings were in September of 1984. "Unlike Americans, who seem to drive everywhere, Russians always walk, especially in the area of Plummer Park where they lived," she said. Although the prosecution had told them that Russian "Third Wave" immigrants could never return home, Pollock said the defense would show that exceptions were made. "During the course of this trial, you will hear that individuals have returned to Russia who emigrated in the 1970s — there are ways of doing this."

Continuing her opening statement, she told the jury, "Nikolai Ogorodnikov is a Russian émigré. He was outspoken about the fact that he missed Russia. He missed his homeland. You must accept that fact and judge his actions as you would any other émigré who came to the United States. As you hear the evidence, you must try to understand that just because someone misses his original homeland does not mean that he would be willing to betray a country that took him in and gave him a home. "Because you will hear so little testimony about Nikolai Ogorodnikov," she concluded, "my remarks to you now are very short. During the course of this trial, you will not hear me ask many questions of most of the witnesses, because most of the witnesses have nothing to say about Nikolai Ogorodnikov."

With that, the first day of Nikolai and Svetlana's trial was over. She was taken back to Sybil Brand, just a few blocks away, while he had the hour-long bus ride to Terminal Island, where all he had to look forward to was the hot meal that Judge Kenyon had made sure he was getting at least once a day. "I was allowed to call Matthew on the telephone, but what could I tell him? That his mother would go to jail for the rest of her life?" he says. "So all we talked about was school, and how nice it would be when we were together again."

Chapter 7

TRIAL AND ERROR

THE very first witness called by the prosecution on April 24, 1985, in the case of the *United States of America v. Nikolai and Svetlana Ogorodnikov* was Mischa Makarian, owner of the popular restaurant and cabaret on Sunset Boulevard in Hollywood where members of the Russian community liked to congregate. He said that both of the Ogorodnikovs were customers, but that more often Svetlana had come in by herself or with friends. Several times she had introduced him to people from the Soviet film industry, and to officials from the Consulate in San Francisco, Makarian told the jury. One of them, Gennady Prishchepa, had even given him his business card, which was introduced as evidence.

Svetlana was not an ideal customer, Makarian testified: she drank too much and made loud pro-Russian statements, often saying she regretted not being able to go back. In her cross-examination, Randy Sue Pollock got Makarian to make the point that Nikolai was quiet compared with Svetlana, and also that many Russian émigrés talked fondly about life in Russia.

Gregory Shenderovsky, a beltmaker from Kiev and a "Third Wave" Russian immigrant who had been in Los Angeles for seven years, testified that he had known Nikolai in Kiev and had met him again in 1978 at the Oriental Theater in Hollywood where Nikolai was taking tickets for a Russian film show. Back at their Gardner Street apartment, Shenderovsky went on, Nikolai began to criticize America. "He says to me, 'I think you make a mistake to come to this country.'" Shenderovsky also said that Nikolai had told him he was trying to earn his way home by showing Russian films. Randy Pollock then established that Nikolai had also talked about the difficulty of getting used to the way of life in America, and she got Shenderovsky to agree that it was true for him, too.

Through an interpreter, a Russian woman named Karine Matevossian — the wife of a Soviet diplomat who had defected with her to Belgium in 1978 — testified that shortly after she arrived in Los Angeles in 1979, Svetlana Ogorodnikova and another woman visited her several times, once accompanied by Soviet officials, and tried to get her to return to Russia.

Then the prosecution's first star witness, retired FBI agent John Hunt, took the stand. A calm and professorial man in his late fifties, Hunt gave the jury his impressive background: two years as a U.S. Treasury Department agent, four years with U.S. Naval Intelligence, then fourteen years with the FBI until a heart condition forced him to retire just two weeks after Richard Miller and the Ogorodnikovs were arrested. Hunt told how he had first met Svetlana on June 18, 1980, when she was questioned after having been followed while driving Soviet consular official Viktor

Zonov around Los Angeles. He called her in February of 1982 to see if she had any interest in becoming an FBI informant. At first she said she wasn't interested, but then in May she called and said she would think it over.

On May 26, 1982, Hunt testified, he and Svetlana met in the Sears parking lot on Sunset Boulevard in Hollywood. Sitting in his car, they talked about various people at the San Francisco Soviet Consulate. She told him how she had been instructed to find Karine Matevossian, and said she had often passed along to the Consulate the business cards of FBI agents who questioned her. At the end of the meeting, Hunt said, she began to cry. "I don't know why I talk to you. Don't call me again or I'll call my lawyer," she told him.

Less then a week later, Hunt went on, she called him again and asked to meet. He took her to dinner at a restaurant called Yesterdays, in Westwood, and then — at her insistence — stopped at a nightclub called Simply Blues in Hollywood for a drink. In the nightclub, Hunt said, she asked him to accept a gift — a Russian doll, one of several she had in a briefcase with her. And outside on the street, Hunt continued, she suddenly threw her arms around him and said, "I love you. Can't we go someplace?"

At this point, Svetlana rose from her seat at the defense table and cried out to Hunt, "Why you lie? Liar!" Her lawyers quickly restrained her.

Looking only slightly shaken, Hunt continued his testimony. When he had turned down her offer of sex, he told the jury, Svetlana said, "If you won't take me, I'm

98

going to find someone who will." He followed her home, worried that she'd had too much to drink, and watched as she drove instead to Mischa's and went inside.

"Mr. Hunt," prosecutor Kendall asked, "did you ever at any time reciprocate Mrs. Ogorodnikova's romantic advances in any way?"

"No, I did not," Hunt answered.

"And did you ever, as Mrs. Ogorodnikova apparently suggested, go some place with her to have sexual intercourse?"

"No, I did not," Hunt repeated.

During four days of intensive cross-examination, Svetlana's lawyer Gregory Stone failed to shake either Hunt's story or his composure. The closest thing to intimacy that Stone was able to elicit from Hunt was the admission of a Russian-style kiss on both cheeks at several meetings with Svetlana, and the possibility that he once put both arms around her when they danced in public.

On May 7, under redirect examination by prosecutor Kendall, Hunt told how Svetlana had telephoned his supervisor, P. Bryce Christensen, in July of 1983 and made a number of startling charges. "She said that I had threatened to kill her," Hunt testified. "She told him that my daughter and I had taken money from her under some type of duress. She told my supervisor that I had promised to leave my wife and run away with her. She complained that my wife was constantly bothering her and begging her to leave her husband alone. She said that she had just returned from Moscow, where she had been sleeping with Premier Andropov."

Earlene Hunt, called as a prosecution witness, testified that she had been married to John Hunt for thirty-three years. She recalled that on the night of June 6, 1982, he called her from Simply Blues to say that he was having a drink with Svetlana and that he would be home a bit later than he thought. She said that on his return, Hunt told her the story of Svetlana's surprising outburst outside the nightclub. Under cross-examination, Mrs. Hunt told the jury how she had helped her husband choose two gifts for Svetlana — a silk scarf and a pearl necklace — in exchange for the gifts she had given him.

P. Bryce Christensen recalled for the jury the call from Svetlana on July 6, 1983, characterizing it as being full of "rambling complaints." He added that three times during the call, he heard her put down the receiver and say very loudly to someone else, "I'm speaking to the FBI!"

FBI agent Nancy Smith talked about going with Hunt to a meeting with Svetlana in a Hollywood restaurant in October of 1983, at which Svetlana told Hunt that she had lied to the Russians that they were having an affair. Smith said Svetlana apologized for lying, but that she was afraid for her son. "Did you suggest to Mr. Hunt during that meeting that Mrs. Ogorodnikova was pretty?" Svetlana's lawyer Stone asked in his cross-examination. "Yes," Smith said, also affirming that Hunt had agreed with her. "And did Mr. Hunt tell you during this conversation that Mrs. Ogorodnikova's prettiness was fatal?" Stone asked. But before Smith could answer, prosecutor Kendall objected and was sustained.

Alexander Polovets, editor and publisher of the weekly Russian-language newspaper *Almanac*

Panorama, told the jury on May 8 about Russian
Pioneer camps like the one called Artek that Matthew
Ogorodnikov attended. Polovets had been to one when
he was a boy, and his son had gone to one before the
family came to America. The purpose of the camps,
Polovets said, was to make children "dedicated to the
Communist Party — they are surrounded by slogans
from the moment they wake up." He also testified how
he had gone to a concert of Russian performers at
Hollywood High School on July 3, 1983, equipped with
a camera and telephoto lens in case a rumored
demonstration took place. "A friend pointed out a car
parked across the street and said something about this
Ogorodnikov. I saw the car, and a man inside taking
pictures, pointing his camera toward our side of the
street and toward the group of people who were going to
demonstrate against Soviet policy," Polovets said. Using
his telephoto lens, he snapped some pictures of the
man. "When he saw me taking his picture, he pointed
his camera in my direction, and he was taking some
pictures of me."

In her cross-examination, Pollock managed to score a
few points for Nikolai's case by getting Polovets to admit
that he was doing the same thing as Nikolai — taking
pictures of the demonstrators; that his pictures had been
published and could be seen by anyone who bought a
copy of his newspaper; and that some Pioneer camps in
Russia are open to European and American children.

Linda Franusich, who worked as a special operations
assistant for the FBI in San Francisco, then took the
stand, letting the jury — and the world — know for the
first time that the FBI ran at least occasional visual
surveillance operations outside the Soviet Consulate.

She testified that during such a surveillance, everyone who went in or out of the Consulate was logged in, license plate numbers were checked, and people were photographed. Franusich then told how on May 23, 1984, she spotted someone she recognized from a prior surveillance — "a white female, approximately five feet one and one hundred and ten pounds, with blonde hair, wearing a white pantsuit" — leaving the Consulate at about 3:04 P.M. carrying several film canisters and walking north on Baker Street. Asked if she saw that person in the courtroom, Franusich pointed to Svetlana.

Using telephone company records, the prosecution showed that a few minutes later, two collect calls were made from a pay phone at a cheese store on Baker Street to the Ogorodnikovs' phone in Hollywood. Then Franusich testified that she saw Svetlana reenter the Consulate, stay for three minutes, come out and be picked up by a man driving a 1979 Datsun. In an effort to impress the bench with the Government's solid investigating team, a taxi driver named Alexander Nayberg was produced; he testified that on the morning of May 23 he picked Svetlana up at San Francisco Airport in his Yellow Cab, took her to a restaurant on Union Street, and made a deal with her to pick her up again — in his own car this time — at the Soviet Consulate at 4 P.M. and take her back to the airport.

The prosecution's next witness was lawyer Donald Levinson, who told the jury essentially the same story he had told the FBI the day after the Ogorodnikovs were arrested: how he had represented Svetlana in a couple of personal injury suits, how he had tried to set up some deals for Russian films through MGM, and how he had gotten involved in the search for Stanislav Levchenko.

many times confused, correct?" Levinson agreed on all these points. "And did you ever have occasion not to understand sentences that he said to you?"

"Oh yes, many times," Levinson answered.

"Or, also, did you have occasion to misinterpret what he would say to you?"

"Yes."

"Mr. Ogorodnikov cannot read English, can he?" Pollock asked.

"No, he cannot," Levinson replied.

Levinson was bounced back and forth like a tennis ball for the next several hours by both prosecution and defense, but the only new information to emerge from his testimony was that Nikolai had been trying to market a machine that made a sort of meat dumpling. To which Judge Kenyon joked, "I had dumplings today, and they could have used some help from his machine."

Diana Baskevitch of the Beverly International Travel Agency took the stand to testify at some length how she had been handling the Ogorodnikovs' travel needs for several years. Numerous airplane ticket stubs to and from Russia, hotel vouchers from the Russian Intourist agency, and invoices from her to them were put into evidence. Each ticket and trip was laboriously entered on the Government's chart. In cross-examination by Svetlana's lawyers, Baskevitch admitted that she knew that visa application information about the Ogorodnikovs' places of birth — listed as in Yugoslavia — was false. Under redirect examination by Kendall, she also testified that it was her understanding that Svetlana

He said that at a meeting at Mischa's restaura₁
Matthew present but Svetlana absent, Nikolai ł
him how important it was that he locate Levche.
means a lot to him, it means a lot to me. That he
be in trouble, and that I could be in trouble. That ₁
simpatico for me," Levinson testified.

"What was Mr. Ogorodnikov's demeanor when he
these things to you?" prosecutor Merritt asked.
"Like always. Highly excited, agitated, very anima
Levinson replied.

In her cross-examination, Pollock got Levinson
describe the Gardner Street apartment, which he h
visited several times. He said it was "almost barren, ve
little furniture. . . . There were film canisters all over th
living room, and books about Soviet cultural films. . .
It was almost depressing, that type of atmosphere." She
also got him to admit that Nikolai seemed most
interested in finding Levchenko so that the lawsuit
could be filed. "Mr. Ogorodnikov had a lot of faith in you
as an attorney, didn't he?" she asked.
"Yes, he did," Levinson replied.
"And he also considered you a friend, did he not?"
"That's correct," said Levinson.

Pollock then tried to get Levinson to admit that he
had never mentioned, when interviewed by the FBI, tha
Nikolai had told him how important it was that he fin
Levchenko, or that they both could be in trouble if I
didn't. She did get him to say that a client approachi
him on a case like this wasn't in itself unusual. "Niko
isn't an easy person to understand, is he?" she ask
"His English is very broken, is it not? His verb tenses

had a "special arrangement" with the Soviet Embassy in Washington, so that all her visa requests were sent directly there for approval.

A former Russian hockey player named Victor Nechaev, once married to an American woman and living in Los Angeles, next told the jury how he and his partner, Serge Levin, got into the movie business with Svetlana and Nikolai in June of 1984. Nechaev said that he and Levin had loaned Svetlana a thousand dollars against her share of the profits, but that only a part of it had been repaid. He and Levin had also been asked to keep an eye open for Stanislav Levchenko. And on July 25, 1984, Nechaev drove with Svetlana to San Francisco — thus explaining the Motel 6 receipt found after her arrest — to exchange films at the Soviet Consulate. Along the way, he told the jury, she stopped to buy cans of margarita mix, which she drank as they drove. This would prove to be the beverage of choice on another trip to San Francisco a month later. About the only interesting item defense attorney Stone could get from Nechaev in his cross-examination was that when his colleagues Brian and Pollock tried to interview him in the interests of the Ogorodnikovs getting a fair trial, Nechaev told them he didn't care if they got a fair trial — Svetlana still owed him money.

Starting on May 17 and running through the next two weeks, a long line of FBI agents took the stand to go into great detail about their surveillance of the Ogorodnikovs and Miller. Ronald L. Durkin told the jury abut the curious events at the shoe counter at Orbach's, after which Svetlana and Nikolai took a two-hour walk around the neighborhood. "I observed that the two of them would stop periodically, and that Nikolai would be

105

very demonstrative with his hands," Agent Durkin said. In her cross-examination, Pollock got Durkin to agree that in the many times he had him under surveillance, Nikolai always talked with his hands. Pollock also made the point — as she did methodically with each FBI agent — that none of them had ever been close enough to Nikolai or Svetlana to hear what they were saying; that none of them spoke Russian anyway, that nobody had ever suggested using sophisticated microphones to pick up their conversation, that the weather was warm and the apartment was small, and that Russians just like to walk a lot.

Anyone familiar with the Los Angeles freeway system had a good laugh during Brian's cross-examination of Durkin on May 22. Asking about an abortive trip made by Svetlana and Nikolai's New York cousin on September 21, 1984, in search of Miller's house in Lynwood, Brian said, "They appeared to be lost, didn't they?" Durkin agreed, describing how they had driven east on the Santa Monica Freeway and then north on the Long Beach Freeway. "They got to the end of the Long Beach Freeway and did a U-turn and came back all the way south," Durkin said. "They may have been trying a dry-clean move, but they could also have been genuinely lost."

Agent Dwight Melzer told about a time when Nikolai abruptly left his apartment and walked along one side of Gardner Street, looking in the windows of all the parked cars. Pollock made him admit that there was no way he could be sure that Nikolai was looking for FBI agents at the time.

Agent John De Pretoro analyzed for the jury the so-called plain language code, which he said Svetlana and

Grishin used in their phone calls. When Grishin asked, "What shall I convey to your acquaintances?" and Svetlana answered, "Well, I'd like to come by tomorrow at five or six for the films," what she was really saying, according to De Pretoro, was that she was using the films as a pretext to visit the Soviet Consulate. Pollock got him to admit that Nikolai and Svetlana were actually in the film business, and that the "movie director friend" referred to on the tapes might have been a real Russian film director she knew rather than a code word for Richard Miller. With the ball bounced back to his court, prosecutor Kendall got De Pretoro to say that he believed when Svetlana told Grishin "My husband will tell you all about it" she meant that Nikolai would give him all the details of the trip to Warsaw when he came to San Francisco on September 24.

Through the FBI agents' testimony, a picture of the prosaic limits of the Ogorodnikovs' lives began to emerge. Nikolai and Matthew were followed going to Zody's and Von's; the whole family went regularly to Ross Dress-For-Less and K-Mart and Save-More Groceries. Other shopping trips, to Ness Shoes and the Big Man Shop, turned out to less ordinary. The manager of Ness Shoes testified that Richard Miller brought back the burgundy Italian shoes, size 11½, which Svetlana had bought him and tried to change them for another color. But when he learned that the only other color was navy blue, he decided to stick with the burgundy. As to what small-sized Nikolai and Svetlana were seeking in the Big Man Shop on Fairfax Avenue, nobody was able to discover.

Several agents told how Nikolai, dressed in a black baseball cap, black leather jacket, black pants, and brown dress shoes, was observed being picked up by Svetlana and Matthew outside the PSA Terminal at Los Angeles Airport on the afternoon of September 24, 1986, after his trip to San Francisco. While Matthew waited in the car, Nikolai and Svetlana were seen to talk outside on the sidewalk for ten minutes. Then they drove home, stopping for an early dinner at McDonald's and behaving oddly along the way. Nikolai would occasionally slow down to twenty-five miles per hour and peer intently at all the cars that passed him. Once he pulled over into a driveway and again scanned passing traffic, making his FBI tails extremely nervous.

One dramatic highpoint came when FBI Agent Richard B. Otstott of the San Francisco office told about how he got lucky on September 25, 1984. Doing a discreet surveillance on vice consul Grishin as part of their routine, Otstott and his team followed Grishin and some other Russians to San Francisco Airport. They lost Grishin after he left his colleagues to go to the toilet, but Otstott spotted him again in a phone booth at 7:30 P.M. After Grishin left, Otstott copied down the number in the booth. Phone company records later showed a call from that number at that time to (213) 876-3148 — the Ogorodnikovs' phone in Hollywood.

The final FBI witness before the long-awaited appearance of Richard W. Miller was an audio expert named Michael Stuart, who told the jury that it would be "virtually impossible" to get sound recordings of Nikolai and Svetlana in their apartment or on their walks without being noticed. He said the FBI even thought about bugging the trees along the way, but decided the traffic noise would cover up everything else. Pollock hammered away at Stuart as to why the FBI hadn't tried harder to hear what was being said — "If you were so afraid of being noticed, why did you use the same cars for 35 days?" But Stuart wouldn't back down, and everyone else in court seemed to be saving their energies for the big fish waiting to testify next.

Chapter 8

WITNESS FOR THE PROSECUTION

T HE first thing Richard Miller did on taking the stand on June 11, 1985, was to invoke the Fifth Amendment — saying he wouldn't testify unless he was assured that what he said wouldn't be used against him in his own trial. Judge Kenyon, the Government prosecutors, and Miller's lawyers had spent many hours kicking this possibility around, and they were ready for it. Judge Kenyon granted Miller limited immunity, then explained to the jury that even though what he said couldn't be used against him, "he is still required to testify and is still required to tell the truth under oath."

Although nobody knew it at the time, Miller's two weeks of testimony at the Ogorodnikovs' trial would be his only appearance on the witness stand during the entire case, the only chance for him to tell his side of the story in public. The circumstances were less than ideal: prosecutor Merritt treated Miller as a hostile witness, and the lawyers for Nikolai and Svetlana also tried to pick away at his testimony. So there was no lawyer in his corner, ready to leap to his feet with objections or direct the questions in his favor.

The unsympathetic tone was set with Merritt's first question, "Are you awaiting trial on your own charges in this indictment?"

"Unfortunately, yes," Miller answered.

"Your honor, could that word 'unfortunately' be stricken as unresponsive?" Merritt asked, and it was so ordered.

Merritt got Miller to describe his FBI career, including problems he'd had with his supervisors along the way. In 1981, in a letter he wrote to oppose a planned transfer from Riverside to Los Angeles, Miller said he was worried about how his being away from home would affect his already-strained marriage. In 1983 he complained about his street cases being taken away from him when he was assigned to listen to and log electronic surveillance. Merritt then hammered away at Miller's excommunication from the Mormon Church because of adulterous affairs: Did he have one? Yes. Did he have more than one? Yes. Did he have more than one in 1984? Yes. "This particular type of problem persisted until October of 1984, didn't it?" Merritt asked.

"I wasn't very happy about it, and I am sorry about it, but yes, it did," Miller answered.

The litany of job failures continued: Miller testified how he was rated "minimally acceptable" in March of 1984; how in April he was suspended for two weeks without pay and put on probation. "Didn't you break down and cry in the squad room when you were given that two-week suspension?" Merritt asked. Miller said that he probably did. "And isn't it the custom at the Bureau, when somebody is suspended without pay, to have his fellow agents pass around the hat to ease the burden?" Merritt went on.

"I've contributed to many situations like that," Miller replied.

"But it wasn't done for you?"

"No."

Miller told the jury how he felt about working in a windowless room instead of an open office, doing menial work instead of having cases to investigate, when he came back from his suspension in May of 1984: "I was unhappy, but you have to roll with the punches." Again, Merritt asked that the qualifying statement "but you have to roll with the punches" be stricken as unresponsive; again, Judge Kenyon agreed.

Then Merritt began to probe relentlessly into Miller's financial condition: how he owed a Riverside service station $1,000 on credit card charges, and how he finally settled it by giving the owner a car; how ten out of twelve monthly mortgage payments a year were late; how he had asked a fellow agent for a loan of $500, had taken $75 instead, and had paid the man back with a check that bounced; how he had stolen money from his wife's grandmother and from an FBI informant called Mary, by taping over the amount she was signing for and then writing in a larger amount. "Mr. Miller, your financial situation was so bad in September of 1984 that you couldn't even get your car fixed, isn't that a fact?" Merritt asked.

"I never did think our financial condition was as bad as you seem to indicate," Miller answered with some attempt at dignity. "My car needed some work on it, but you have your priorities, and everybody has a budget." Still, Merritt managed to build up a picture of Miller as a man obsessed with the need to make extra money at the time Svetlana entered his life.

Their first meeting took place — after two calls to his office — on May 24, 1984, in a parking lot, where so much of this seedy drama seems to have been played out. This one was at the corner of Westwood and Santa Monica Boulevards, and Svetlana got out of an old, battered car. "Was she driving?" Merritt asked. "I don't think so, because she got out of the car and the car went away. So I assume somebody else was driving," Miller said, earning a laugh from the jury and spectators.

Svetlana was "very distraught," Miller testified. "She said she had to go back to Russia, and was being forced to work with the GRU" — Soviet Military Intelligence. She paid for that first lunch, in Marina del Rey — against FBI policy, as Merritt was quick to point out — as she was to pay for every meal and drink and motel room they subsequently shared. After lunch, he left her in his car in the Federal Building parking lot while he went upstairs to talk to his supervisor about her. Even though he was warned about not having anything to do with her, he went back downstairs and drove with her to Malibu. "We were talking more about her problems and just things in general, about life and how to approach it, how to handle it," Miller said when asked what they had talked about.

On their second date, a week later, they had sex for the first time. "Where?" asked Merritt. "In my car," Miller answered. During this and subsequent testimony about his wife's extracurricular sex life, Nikolai sat alternately angry and disbelieving. "During the trial, he and Svetlana were swearing at each other in Russian under their breaths," Randy Pollock said later. "He also had his head down a lot, as though he couldn't believe what was being said. When they showed a videotape of Svetlana and Miller going at it, he didn't understand what was happening — he had to ask me what was going on."

Miller admitted that he made no written reports on Svetlana, even though he was presumably evaluating her as a possible asset. "Did you ever consider the fact that, excellent asset or not, if it became known that you had a sexual relationship with her, you would probably be fired?" Merritt asked.

"Well, if I thought about that, I wouldn't have done it," Miller answered. "So I don't think I thought about it." And later he said, "The sex just sort of came with the territory. . . sort of a James Bond fantasy."

Miller than described the beginnings of his plan to use Svetlana to help his career. "Of all the areas of my life — the religious aspect, my marital relationship, and my work — the area that seemed I could make the most headway with would be work, because I spent the most time there. So I thought perhaps I could accomplish something that hadn't been accomplished before, and that was to infiltrate, to the best of my ability, the Soviet intelligence service."

He admitted that he had been warned, by both John Hunt and his supervisor Gary Auer, to proceed with caution. Was he doing that, Merritt asked? "Well, I think I was proceeding a little differently than they had perceived, but I wouldn't consider it caution," Miller answered.

Under Merritt's questioning, Miller admitted that he had in fact started a file on Svetlana, but it was a far cry from the detailed document he should have prepared. In his Lynwood house after his confession, the FBI found a folder with "Svetlana" written on the outside. It contained a scrap of paper with the words "Major Micholenkov" — presumably Svetlana's KGB code name; a reading list including John Barron's *KGB Today*; a printout of Svetlana's record from the California Department of Motor Vehicles; another piece of paper with "Husband — Nikolai, born Kiev" written on it, followed by Nikolai's birthdate and date of entry into the United States; some sketchy information obviously taken from Svetlana's existing FBI file — "White female, USSR national, age 34, born 5/10/50, 5 feet, 105 pounds, eyes blue-green." There was also the first page of a typed memo about their first meeting, which ended in midsentence.

On August 2, after he had been warned several more times not to have anything to do with her, Svetlana called him again. He got the message down at the Santa Ana FBI office where he was filling in. "She said, 'Would you like to get together?' and the yellow light went on, that I should proceed with caution," Miller told the jury. "And then I thought, at least she's contacting me. . .well, you know, maybe there's some hope for my objective after all." During the next few weeks, he testified, they had meetings at the Queen Mary in Long Beach, at restaurants in Monterey Park and Malibu, at her apartment, and at his house in Lynwood.

The subject of money first came up at the Chart House in Malibu, Miller told the court. Svetlana wanted a list of FBI personnel for recruitment purposes; "I think she also mentioned something about Bryce Christensen having a safe and that I could get into it. And I said, 'You know, I'm not a burglar; I don't know how to get into stuff like that.' And she said, 'Well, we can provide you with any kind of equipment, stuff like you need.' And I thought to myself, 'There's a live one here!' " It was then that he first mentioned needing to have $50,000 in gold placed in three banks before he would meet anyone, Miller said.

On August 7, they had dinner at a Charlie Brown's restaurant in Rosemead. Svetlana was so drunk, Miller testified, that she went to the bathroom and then couldn't find their table again; he found her wandering around in a daze. After sex in a motel in Hollywood, she asked him if he would like to meet someone that very night. But before the story of the meeting with Nikolai could be told to the jury, there was a long discussion between the judge and the lawyers. The defense contended that since Miller didn't know who Nikolai was at that point, thought he was someone called Wolfson, his evidence should not be admitted. The prosecution made a telling statement when Merritt said they sorely needed Miller's evidence; "If we haven't made a *prima facie* case against Nikolai, he's going to be dismissed out!" Judge Kenyon finally let Miller's evidence stand, and he went on to confirm the defense's contention that most of the conversation that night was on Miller's part. According to his testimony, Nikolai mostly listened, shook his head occasionally, and said "No problem!" several times in heavily-accented English.

When he went back to the FBI office in Westwood at 2 A.M. and discovered that Nikolai Wolfson and Nikolai Ogorodnikov were the same man, Miller said he called Svetlana and told her, "You lied to me. And all this other stuff is a lie, and I don't want to have anything more to

do with you!" Nevertheless, within three days they were
seeing each other again — even going out to a "purely
social" dinner with two other Russian émigrés, Ludmilla
Kondratjeva and Vladimir Ratchikhine. This event
would become interesting, if not important to the case
at hand, several months later when Kondratjeva's body
was pulled out of her white Volkswagen Rabbit in the
Pacific Ocean in Malibu, and her lover Ratchikhine was
found guilty of involuntary manslaughter in her death.

What was Miller's attitude at this point, Merritt
asked. "I was just going with the flow, I had to wait and
see," he answered.

"You wanted to wait and see if the $50,000 turned up
in the bank, isn't that what you wanted to wait and see?"

"That would have been ideal, yes," Miller replied.

"I bet it would," Merritt commented sarcastically, and
got a laugh from the court before defense objections cut
him off.

Miller's direct testimony ended with a new wrinkle in
the story of how Svetlana took his badge and ID card
into the Soviet Consulate. Miller now insisted that he
hadn't given her the items at all; she had taken them
from his ditty bag, where he kept them because the
jogging suit he was wearing had no pockets. Merritt
ended his examination without getting an answer to his
question about whether Miller had sent in his
credentials with a note from him, handwritten on motel
stationery, as he had first told one of the FBI agents who
questioned him.

Brad Brian began his cross-examination of Miller on
June 20 by attempting to establish that at each of their
first three meetings Svetlana had not asked for any

professional information about the FBI, and that Miller had tried to project himself as being potentially recruitable. Then he went into a lengthy discussion of Miller's FBI problems. At one point, Miller became emotional about the possibility of his being fired: "Well, I could always get a job. In fact, I would have welcomed being fired." Then reality set in; he admitted that he didn't really want to be fired, "but at least it would have given me another direction and maybe help me regroup myself and put my life back together. But I didn't aspire to it. I only had a couple of more years to retire. That is what I was sort of working for."

Then Brian went to work on the discrepancies between what Miller first told Bryce Christensen after he decided to bare his soul, and what later came out under more intense FBI grilling. For example, he had never told Christensen about the August 7 meeting with Nikolai, had he? No, Miller agreed, but that first statement to Christensen was more of an "overview" than a list of every single thing that happened.

Wasn't it a fact that Miller had lied to Svetlana about his responsibilities at the FBI? "I wasn't about to tell her what I really did," Miller replied. How come Miller had never used a body recorder when he was with Svetlana? "If I had, I would have been undone," was his answer. And then he added, "Conducting a maverick investigation, I really wasn't in a position to do such a thing." And hadn't Miller lied to Svetlana when he told her that he was replacing John Hunt as her FBI contact? "On the way back from San Francisco, when we were arguing, she was saying, 'Who's next? Who's next? First it's Hunt and then it's you! Who's next?' And I said, 'I'm it — I'm sure there's not going to be anybody behind me.' "

During Brian's cross-examination, Miller admitted that he had been drinking "for the first time in my life" on the trip to San Francisco, that Svetlana bought canned margarita mix and cognac at various stops along the way. Brian also tried without much success to get Miller to agree that when Svetlana said "I know this heart — it is my job," she might possibly have been referring to some EKG training she had taken for her job as a nurse's aide. Asked why they had rushed away from the Café Casino that time without eating, Miller answered, "I think she wanted some Chicken McNuggets."

As to the question of who had been persuading who to go to Vienna, Brian asked, "Selling is one of your skills, isn't it, Mr. Miller?"

"Yes, I enjoy selling," Miller answered. He also admitting to saying to his wife on October 1, "Well, I'm so used to lying, one more just isn't going to make a difference."

Then it was Randy Pollock's turn to try using Miller's testimony to Nikolai's advantage. She began by getting him to say that Svetlana had told him she was unhappy with her husband, that they were separated, that she was distressed because her son was closer to his father than to her. "I wasn't sure what Nikolai did for a living," Miller then admitted. "It didn't seem to very important."

"You never asked her what he did for a living?" Pollock queried.

"We never talked about her husband, hardly at all," Miller replied. Nor had John Hunt ever mentioned Nikolai to him. "I had much more background and general information about her and her activities; he didn't seem to even be involved." Nikolai's FBI index card,

121

Miller went on, contained nothing more than his name and his alias, Nikolai Wolfson.

On that night of August 7, Pollock asked, wasn't it true that with Nikolai in his bathrobe "it definitely looked like he did not expect company at that time?" Miller agreed, then described their conversation: "I think he started to say some things, but his English was so bad. I think, on my part, I tended to just sort of review what I had said, or what Svetlana and I had discussed, so that he virtually just sort of agreed. See, I was assuming I was meeting somebody of great import. So I assumed that he sort of already knew what was happening." All Nikolai really said in their six- or seven-minute encounter, Miller admitted, was "Yah, yah, yah" — which he took to mean "No problem."

When Pollock had finished with Miller, prosecutor Merritt took over for a few more questions, trying hard to get him to link Nikolai to Svetlana. "Did Mrs. Ogorodnikova ever tell you anything about Mr. Ogorodnikov's meetings with you?" Merritt asked. "No," Miller answered. Then he said, "I had no understanding that he had any involvement. She seldom talked about her husband or what he did."

After the meeting, Miller said, he raced back to the FBI office to check the files because "it certainly didn't correlate with any spy thriller I had ever read." Seeing Nikolai's card, he felt, "I had been lied to again; anything that Nikolai and I had discussed was a joke. It was of no value. I had struck out again." And wasn't it true, Pollock asked, that after August 8 he never gave any more thought to Nikolai Ogorodnikov? "No," Miller admitted. "I just sort of chalked it up as a bad experience."

Under normal circumstances, Miller's testimony should have been a strong plus, at least for Nikolai's case. But, as everyone was about to discover, circumstances in the matter of Nikolai and Svetlana Ogorodnikov were far from normal.

Chapter 9

Bending Under the Pressure

WHEN the jury arrived for its half-day session on June 25, 1985, they found the court in a state of barely-repressed excitement. Rumors were buzzing through the aisles that something was up, and when Judge Kenyon sent the jury home for the day because of a "problem that just has to be resolved," the buzzing only increased in volume.

What happened was that morning the Government had offered Svetlana and Nikolai a deal: plead guilty now and you'll get a lighter sentence than if you make us take it all the way to the end. It wasn't the first plea bargain that had been proposed; "At one point, the Government offered to let us plead no contest, which would have meant very little jail time for Nikolai," says Randy Pollock. "We would have gone with that, but the prosecutors were getting severe pressure from Washington and called it off." But this latest offer had one major condition: both parties had to plead guilty or it was no deal.

126

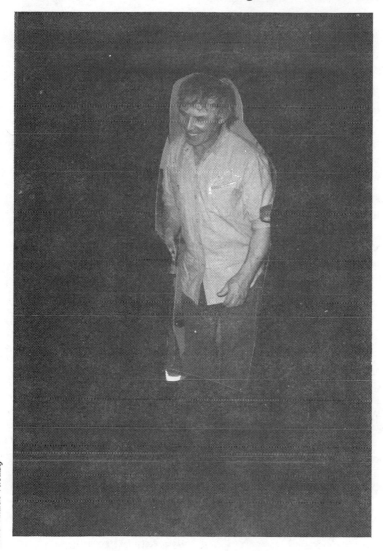

Spies don't only hurt their country; they also hurt those who love them most — their children.

"They came to me, Svetlana's lawyers, and they say, 'Nikolai, we're losing this case. If you don't plead guilty, she gets life in prison.' I say, 'What I have to do?' He say, 'You have to do this if she is to have any life left.' I say, 'Tell me what I have to do! Teach me what I have to say!' I know very well what is happening; the Government wants to convict me and keep me forever with my mouth shut. I tell Randy, 'You think I don't understand why they do it? They're afraid that I'll be out in the streets saying how they should never have convicted this woman! This is why I was never called as a witness," says Nikolai now.

"The only way Svetlana could get off with eighteen years instead of a life sentence was for Nikolai to accept eight years as part of a package deal," says Pollock. "The Government wouldn't let him stand trial alone, and they would never sever him from her because it was espionage, and nobody has ever been acquitted of espionage in this country. Svetlana's lawyers were pressuring him to accept, and she was crying and pleading with him, so he caved in. I wouldn't let him plead guilty until he actually admitted he'd done something, so he told me that he did know some of the things she was doing and had given her some advice."

At 12:30 the next afternoon, June 26, while the jury still waited in the wings, prosecutor Kendall rose and announced to Judge Kenyon, "Your Honor, the parties have agreed on a disposition of the case, and the disposition will involve pleas of guilty by both of the defendants in this case." Those journalists who had an early deadline nearly knocked each other over as they broke for the door and the press-room telephones. "Now please, everybody, I don't want people roaring around out there!" Judge Kenyon cautioned.

Kenyon then explained that, under Rule 11, he was obliged to listen to statements from and ask questions of both defendants to prove that they really understood what was going on. He ran down a long list of their constitutional rights and how their guilty pleas affected those rights. "Now, having discussed these several rights with you, do you still wish to plead guilty?" Kenyon asked. "Mrs. Ogorodnikova?"

"Yes," Svetlana answered.

"How about you, sir?"

"I am guilty, maybe," Nikolai answered in Russian, through the court interpreter.

"The point is, you have heard your rights," Judge Kenyon persisted. "Do you still wish to plead guilty?"

"Guilty? I don't know. I explain everything to you what I remember. This time you got decision whether I am guilty or not. I think I am guilty," Nikolai said.

Judge Kenyon next made sure that both defendants understood their sentences. Then he asked an important question, and seemed not to hear or understand Nikolai's answer. "Has anyone threatened you or forced you in any way to plead guilty today?" Svetlana, subdued and docile, answered "No." Nikolai's reply was a cryptic "My conscience is forcing me to say that." Kenyon swept on to the next point, whether any promises had been made other than the ones mentioned so far. Both gave straight "No" answers to that.

Now it was time for Nikolai to make his statement of guilt, in response to Judge Kenyon's question, "Did you have anything to do with the conspiracy, and if you did, what was your part in it?"

"If you start from the very beginning, just that I lived with Svetlana," Nikolai said as he started what would be a long, rambling, emotional statement — his only chance to stand up in court and have his say. "And Svetlana told me somewhere in the month of May that an FBI person was calling her; he says he has something to tell her of a serious nature. I said, 'Why do you need to find work for yourself? Why are you going to get involved with him?' She told me, 'I am just going to see him and come back just one time.'

"Then in August, she very frequently would come home drunk. I am sitting at home late many nights with Matthew, with my son. He is worried, and so am I. I tried to explain it to him; 'I think she's got a boyfriend.' One night she came home very late and very drunk. She said she had something to explain to me if we walked downstairs. Then she told me that this FBI agent asked her to introduce him to some Soviet agents."

Trying to move things along, Judge Kenyon agreed to Pollock's suggestion that she ask Nikolai a few key questions. On the subject of the trip to Vienna, she asked, "Did you give her any information as to how the trip should proceed, who should carry the documents?"

"She asked me. She just asked me. I told her — I just gave her advice," Nikolai answered.

"What advice did you give her?"

"I gave advice and said, 'You cannot take any documents. If you think to go, my advice to you as far as what you are telling me and as far as I can believe you, is that this is a big risk for you. Let him go. They can arrest you right here in the airport."

"Did you ever tell her not to go with the agent to Vienna?" Pollock asked.

"I didn't directly," Nikolai replied. "I didn't say 'Don't go to Vienna' concretely because my relationship with her was already not strong enough that I could have an influence on her. Therefore, I just gave her advice that it wasn't worth it."

"Did you tell her he should carry the documents and not her?"

"That is correct," Nikolai answered, seemingly glad of something concrete he could finally admit to. "I said that. Yes. Sure. She shouldn't take any documents with her. I told her that because — because she is the mother of my child. I had to tell her."

"Did you discuss with her on the walks that she was planning to go to Vienna with the agent?" Pollock persisted.

"Yes, she told me. She told me that she wants to. She is planning to go with him. She told me," Nikolai replied.

Judge Kenyon then asked Nikolai some questions of his own. Was there going to be a representative of the Russian government at this meeting in Vienna? "Absolutely. Sure," Nikolai told him. Did he know anything about any money that was going to pass? "I heard about it that he was talking about money, of course," Nikolai admitted. He also told about being taken along while Svetlana bought the burgundy shoes for Miller, and explained the trip to the Big Man Shop: "She said she wanted to buy him some cheap raincoat. I said, 'Go ahead and buy it.'"

When Merritt asked if Nikolai had ever advised Svetlana on what flights to take to Vienna, his reply

131

was, "I just asked about cheaper tickets." What about all the stopping and slowing down in the car coming back from the airport after his trip to San Francisco? "Yes, yes," agreed Nikolai. "I stop my car. I know somebody check me. Because my son tell me about all the time car looking at us. So I stop, I check what's happening, I go again."

Finally, Merritt asked Nikolai about a telephone call made on October 1, 1984, from a booth at the State Employment Office in Hollywood. The call was to Richard Miller at the FBI office in Westwood. "I remember this, everything," Nikolai said. "Before picking up my boy at school, I walk around with my wife. She said she has to make a call. I found booth at Employment Office. She told me the number and asked me to dial it for her, and when someone will answer I should give the phone to her." Did he know who she was calling? "No. She asked for some name. I have an idea she was calling just prior to this trip, probably the agent. I didn't know Miller. I didn't know his last name at all."

Judge Kenyon asked prosecutor Kendall which admissions of Nikolai's he thought constituted a factual basis for a guilty plea. "The primary admissions would be that the defendant was aware that Mrs. Ogorodnikova was to travel to Europe, and that he was aware that the caller from the Consulate had requested that they go to Warsaw; that he knew that Mrs. Ogorodnikova and Mr. Miller, who he did not know by name but knew as an FBI agent, were at least going to Vienna. That the purpose of the trip was for Mr. Miller and Mrs. Ogorodnikova to meet with Soviet representatives, and for Mr. Miller to deliver documents to these representatives in return for being paid large sums of money. That he knew this proposed trip was illegal, and that he gave Mrs. Ogorodnikova advice on how to accomplish the trip successfully," Kendall replied.

There was some discussion about the trip to Ness Shoes, with Judge Kenyon finally agreeing it was relevant because, as Kendall said, "it was an overt act to participate in the purchase of the shoes; and half the money that was paid for the shoes was his money, because they are husband and .wife." The only victory Pollock won was an admission from the prosecution that Nikolai's trip to the Consulate on September 24 was solely for the purpose of exchanging films.

"Is there anything further at this point?" Judge Kenyon asked Nikolai.

"This is everything. This is complete. This is completed already," he answered. "Because all that is important stuff mixed up in it. Maybe it would be a little clearer, but I said enough already so that you would understand that I feel I am guilty of something."

Judge Kenyon agreed, accepted Nikolai's guilty plea, and then asked him if he wanted to be sentenced right away or wait for a presentencing report, which could affect his parole chances, as Svetlana had already indicated she wanted to do. Nikolai insisted he wanted to be sentenced right away. Pollock asked Judge Kenyon to have the sentence read that Nikolai would be eligible for parole after two years; Merritt argued that no special eligibility for parole was deserved. "I don't think his statements here today have been accurately portraying his role in this conspiracy," Merritt said. "I believe the jury would have found that his role was more substantial than he was prepared to admit."

Nikolai, who had been becoming more and more agitated as the proceedings went on, finally exploded. "I did everything so as to help her!" he told the court in a choked voice. "I did everything that was required of me — even more than was required of me. I became a sacrifice...I had to sacrifice, and I am not guilty of anything here. I am in a corner if they are going to say that. I don't want her to stay forever in prison. But if you are going to be cheap about this parole, then it wasn't even worth saying this. I knew that I could win this case here. I knew that I was sacrificed because she was a drunk. She drank her whole life, and everything that happened came from that."

Judge Kenyon interrupted to ask if Nikolai was taking back his guilty plea. "I am saying that I am guilty according to the law that you consider," Nikolai replied. "But you have to understand my feelings inside. I did everything that was required of me. I am not worried about parole. I sat in prison for fifteen years in the Soviet Union, and I sat in the German prison. I am not afraid of American prison. But what I am saying now is that I didn't plan any actions. I didn't perform any actions. I just said everything so as to help her, to take her away from the dangerous road.

"I was offended because the prosecutor stood up and tried to make this whole thing cheap with his talk of two years or not two years. If you grant the parole earlier, I appreciate it very much, because you understand my situation. I lost my son. I lost my wife. Who raped my wife? FBI agents. But they are safe under the American flag. They used the American system, they took my wife, used her as a prostitute, and I ended up outside like a dog. So now you are going to be cheap about these two years, as to whether they are going to give me parole or not. It is just the principle. I understand everything, and I will go through the parole twice. That is just not nice."

Judge Kenyon thanked Nikolai for his statement and then proceeded to do exactly as Merritt had requested — sentence Nikolai to eight years, with no special eligibility for early parole.

By contrast, Svetlana's admission of guilt went very smoothly. Brian read out her statement — that virtually everything the Government charged her with was true — and she just said "Yes" quietly at various points until it was done. Perhaps more emphasis was placed on Miller's influence than the facts warranted, but he wasn't on trial as yet. No one else had anything to add, so Judge Kenyon quickly accepted the guilty plea and set sentencing for a later date — although nobody expected him to change the eighteen years agreed on by both parties.

When the jury was finally called in, about 3 P.M., they heard from Judge Kenyon what the rest of the world could already have learned by listening to their radios — that guilty pleas had been offered and accepted. Kenyon released the jury, thanked them for their efforts, and asked them not to talk to the press because of the upcoming trial of Richard Miller. "You have absolutely no obligation to talk to the media," Kenyon assured them, "but you have absolutely no restraints upon you to keep you from talking to them." Kenyon then closed the proceedings by praising the lawyers for both sides. "If I had a daughter or a son who wanted to be a lawyer and came home and told me that they wanted to work for any one of you, I would think they got a very good deal," he said.

But the case wasn't really over. Back at Terminal Island, where he was to stay through the Miller trial, Nikolai began to have second thoughts about what he had just done. "The officers who watch over me twenty-four hours a day, who watch TV with me, they all say to me, 'Why you plead guilty? Never plead guilty!'" he remembers. "I say to them, 'What I can do? People pressuring me — my wife getting life in prison if I do not. It looks like I am chicken! I can't leave this woman to rot in jail — I just can't!'" But during the next few days, as the injustice of what had happened to him began to sink in, he decided to fight. He told Randy Pollock at several meetings that he wanted to appeal. She had already given notice that she was leaving the Federal Public Defender's Office, but she agreed to file one last motion on his behalf.

The motion, stating that Nikolai was innocent of all the charges and that he had said he was guilty only because of the pressure exerted by the Government and Svetlana's lawyers, hit Judge Kenyon's desk on July 29. The surprised judge appointed a private lawyer, Terry Amdur, to represent Nikolai and to determine whether he had legal grounds to withdraw his guilty plea. As they waited for Judge Kenyon to make a decision on the appeal which Amdur soon filed for, lawyers on both sides couldn't help wondering what effect this might have on Svetlana's own plea bargain, and on the Miller trial to come.

Chapter 10

MILLER'S TIME

A nervous Richard Miller awaits the jury's verdict — was he a bumbling and misguided FBI agent? Or, was he a traitor scheming to betray his country?

A WEEK after Nikolai dropped his bombshell, Richard Miller's first trial began. (In Norfolk, Virginia, that same week, the Government was also cranking up the first of the trials in the Walker family/U.S. Navy spy case.) The prosecution, headed by U.S. Attorney Robert Bonner and Assistant U.S. Attorney Russell Hayman, and Miller's defense team of Stanley Greenberg and Joel Levine, had already spent three weeks selecting a six-man, six-woman jury. If either side had any worries about the jury or the trial, Judge Kenyon's ongoing gag order kept them from sharing them with the press and public.

Bonner's opening statement set the harsh tone for the prosecution's case, a tone that would remain unsoftened in the months ahead. Richard Miller was a bumbler, a liar, and a cheat, Bonner told the jury. But much worse than all of these, Miller was a traitor to his job and to his country — a danger to security and an embarrassment to the FBI. Bonner ran through the charges against Miller, and how the Government would prove each one. Then he came to the crucial day of September

140

FBI Agent Richard Miller

26, 1984 — the day of the Westwood shopping trip and the Burberry and the reported realization by Miller in the Little League parking lot that the FBI had him under surveillance. "By this point in time, Miller had doubts he could get away with it," Bonner told the jury. "He decided to cut his losses and give the FBI his bail-out story. But don't be fooled — Richard Miller was pursuing his own venal scheme and not the interests of the FBI or his country."

In the defense's three-hour opening statement, Stanley Greenberg conceded that Miller's intelligence, job performance, and moral behavior were seriously flawed. "I don't want to embarrass Mr. Miller, but as an FBI agent he had a far lower level of intelligence than his job required," Greenberg said. He was also an admitted adulterer and cheat. Then he went on to describe how this below-average FBI agent, "more like Jackie Gleason in *The Honeymooners* than Efrem Zimbalist, Jr. in *The FBI*," actually had managed to do what better-qualified agents couldn't. Holding up a large color photo of Soviet vice consul Aleksandr Grishin, Greenberg told the jury that "the fish was on the hook; he wasn't in the boat yet, but he was on the hook," that Miller had managed to use Svetlana Ogorodnikova to persuade Grishin and other KGB officials that he was ready to be recruited. "Every coin has two sides and every story has two versions," Greenberg concluded. "Virtually everything you see and hear in this trial is going to be a two-edged sword. You are going to have to decide what was in Mr. Miller's mind. Keep an open mind. Wait until you've heard it all."

During a break in the trial, Paula Miller was allowed to speak briefly with her husband, but she was rapidly escorted out of the courtroom after Bonner said he didn't want her seen by the jury because she might be called as a defense witness. Outside the court, Mrs. Miller complained about the treatment she and her family were getting from the Government. "Mr. Bonner doesn't want any humanizing element in this case," she told reporters. "He doesn't want the jury to know that our son, Drew, is deaf because of a disease he caught while were stationed in Puerto Rico, or that I'm here and would like to be in the courtroom with my husband."

The prosecution began its case by calling witnesses to testify about Miller's character. As Donna Generaux was telling the jury how she had trouble collecting the monthly payments on the $130,000 Bonsall property that she had sold Miller and his in-laws in 1976, her husband, Glenn, startled the crowded courtroom by leaping to his feet and shouting, "I don't need a microphone to tell this court that Mr. Miller's financial difficulties don't mitigate in any way what he did!" Glenn Generaux was quickly ejected by Federal marshals. Outside the courtroom, he told reporters, "We need the death penalty." It turned out later that Generaux had warned the press earlier that "there's going to be some shouting around here."

Week two began with some surprising testimony from Gary Auer, head of the Soviet counterintelligence squad at the FBI's Los Angeles office and Miller's immediate superior. Auer told the jury that a psychiatric evaluation of Miller in 1982, showing him to be under severe stress and possibly on the verge of a mental breakdown, was the reason why he had been reassigned to the sensitive counterintelligence squad in the first place. "That statement by the psychiatrist was a factor in my decision to

143

take Miller off the street," Auer said. "I wished to assign Mr. Miller to matters that wouldn't put any undue pressure on him." Auer also testified, under cross-examination from Greenberg, that after Miller reported a contact with Svetlana Ogorodnikova in May of 1984, he briefly considered reopening Svetlana's informant file and letting Miller work with her. But he said that John Hunt had convinced him this was a bad idea.

Then it was Hunt's turn to take the stand. Still the picture of calm efficiency, the retired FBI agent told the crowded courtroom how he had warned Miller against getting involved with Svetlana. He said that Miller first told him in May of 1984 that Svetlana had called and offered to provide information about the Russian community in Los Angeles. She didn't want to be identified as the source of the information, Miller told Hunt, so she proposed to use a friend called Sasha as a conduit. Sasha expected to be paid for his services. "I told Miller that Svetlana probably owed this Sasha some money, and she was trying to use the FBI to settle her debt," Hunt testified. "I said to him, 'R.W., she's smarter than both of us. You're really getting in over your head.'"

During the next several weeks, Hunt testified, he asked Miller if Svetlana had called him back. "Each time he said, 'Not yet.' I always told him, 'Don't worry — she'll call.'"

On August 24, salesman Mark White recalled for the court what had happened eleven months before, on September 26, 1984, when Miller and Svetlana walked into the At Ease men's clothing store in Westwood where he worked. They struck him as a very odd couple, he said, and they seemed in quite a hurry to buy a top-of-the-line Burberry trench coat. White, who pointed out Miller sitting at the defense table, remembered that the customer needed a size 50 long. "He was a bit less than six feet tall, but his height was influenced by his girth," White recalled. "He was a bit heavy set."

The so-called Mormon Connection surfaced as Bryce Christensen, assistant agent in charge of the FBI's Los Angeles office, admitted that he had told Miller he was transferred from Riverside to Los Angeles because he needed closer supervision and because he and Christensen were both Mormons. Christensen also told the court about Miller's meetings with Richard Bretzing, special agent in charge of the Los Angeles FBI office and a Mormon bishop, just before his arrest. Christensen said that Bretzing had urged Miller to "consider the moral and spiritual consequences" of committing espionage against the United States. Under cross-examination by Joel Levine, Christensen told of the session between Bretzing and Miller on September 29, 1984. "Mr. Bretzing talked about the process of repentance and the necessity of restitution," Christensen testified. "By the 'process of repentance,' do you mean a type of action within the Mormon Church?" Levine asked him. "Yes, I do," Christensen answered. "Next day, Mr. Bretzing asked Mr. Miller if he had thought over their conversation. At that time, Mr. Miller came forward voluntarily about his association with Mrs. Ogorodnikova, and Mr. Bretzing told him that if he had done what the allegations said he had done, he should consider telling the Government so that a damage assessment could be made," Christensen testified.

Bretzing himself later took the stand and, often becoming visibly angry under cross-examination by Stanley Greenberg, insisted that his urging of Miller to confess was strictly for reasons of security rather than religion. "My concern was that I knew Mr. Miller had access to extremely sensitive information which could have endangered national defense, jeopardized ongoing investigations, and placed the lives of people working for the U.S. Government in jeopardy," Bretzing testified.

Did you have any concerns about your own career when you pressed Miller to confess?" asked Greenberg, referring to reports that Bretzing had been under fire for the way the Los Angeles office of the FBI handled recent cases. "I'm concerned about my career, and I have been for twenty-five years," Bretzing answered.

On September 5, a woman who said she had a short love affair with Miller at the same time as he was seeing Svetlana surprised Miller's lawyers by testifying that he called her collect on the day of his arrest, told her he was in trouble, and then confessed that he had passed "one" confidential document to the Russians. Marta York, a thirty-six-year-old Salvadorian immigrant and mother of five now working as a waitress in Portland, Oregon, said she had first met Miller in 1970, when he and her husband became friends. When her husband died in June of 1984, York said that Miller called and told her he was divorced. He invited her to Los Angeles for a two-week vacation in September, during which time they had a brief sexual liaison, and he tried to borrow two hundred dollars from her so that he could join a health club to lose weight.

Even though she found out that Miller had lied about being divorced, York said she still felt "affection" for him,

146

and was upset when he called to tell her he was in trouble "before you read about it in the newspapers." As York collapsed in tears, Miller's lawyers pointed out that there was no hint of any such confession in her previous interviews with the FBI. During subsequent cross-examination, York admitted that she had told several contradictory versions of the same story, but insisted that the present one was the truth as she remembered it.

The Government then introduced evidence, which it said proved that Miller had indeed passed a secret document to Svetlana. This included a large blow-up of a map of his Lynwood house, reportedly drawn by Miller during his five-day interrogation to show where he had first handed Ogorodnikova a copy of *Reporting Guidance: Foreign Intelligence Information.* FBI agent Larry E. Torrence also testified that Miller had confessed to slipping another copy of the document into Svetlana's bag just before she entered the Soviet Consulate in San Francisco with his badge and ID.

Richard A. Larkin, a retired major general in the U.S. Army who had once served as head military attaché in Moscow, took the stand on September 10 to testify about how the document that Miller supposedly passed to the Russians could have caused critical damage to national security. Without going into detail about the still-secret booklet, Larkin said it "sets forth nearly every area of U.S intelligence needs and requirements. If it fell into Soviet hands, it would give them a chance to take steps to keep U.S. intelligence agents from finding out what the U.S. Government needed to know. The Soviets could establish countermeasures once they knew what we're after." Larkin said that the booklet was also dangerous because the questions not included "would tip the Soviets to information that the U.S. Government knows, possibly revealing U.S. sources and endangering their lives." He also said it would give the Soviets a chance to feed false information to U.S. agents. "It betrays the questions we are asking," he testified.

The next day, the prosecution began its attack on Miller's story about trying to use Svetlana to infiltrate the KGB. David Major, director of intelligence and counterintelligence for the National Security Council — who taught a class on how to work with foreign agents, which Miller attended in 1982 — told the court that any FBI agent trying to infiltrate the KGB "would have to reveal so much secret information to prove he was legitimate that it wouldn't be worth the effort." Major testified that such an agent trying to convince a foreign government's intelligence service that he wanted to work for them "would have to produce intelligence — classified intelligence — before that service would respond in a positive manner. The gains are not going to outweigh the losses."

Major also testified that all double-agent operations have to be approved in advance, as must any classified documents passed to foreign intelligence to prove a source's credibility. But under cross-examination by Joel Levine, Major seemed to weaken the prosecution's case when he testified that, in his experience, Soviet agents working in the United States never used sex and blackmail to compromise U.S. agents.

John Barron, author of two books on the KGB, was the prosecution's next witness, and he contradicted Major on the subject of sex. "Sexual relations involve certain intimacies which the recruiting agent will try to transfer into the mental and political sphere," Barron testified. "The Soviets call this pillow talk. The agent is able to recruit the target in the bedroom." Barron told of Western diplomats who were recruited through sex and intrigue, and said the recruitment of FBI agents is "of transcendent importance to the KGB because the FBI is the first line of defense in the United States against such clandestine activities."

Barron testified that Soviet goals weren't simply a quest for classified documents; "they are looking for lifetime spies — vulnerable agents they can exploit. They're looking for a person with financial difficulties, poor judgment, sexual promiscuity, social isolation, and career frustration."

U.S. Attorney Bonner asked Barron what might happen if an FBI agent met with KGB officials in a foreign country. "They would wring him dry of all information he had — everything he knows," Barron answered. "It's very likely that they would send him back to the FBI as an 'agent-in-place,' an agent working full time for the KGB."

Then, to the surprise of a jammed courtroom, which had been expecting to hear some steamy testimony from Svetlana, the prosecution announced that it was resting it case without calling her or Nikolai. Miller's lawyers immediately asked for a dismissal of all charges against him, saying that in six weeks of prosecution testimony there was no direct evidence against him other than his own statements to the FBI. Judge Kenyon rejected the defense plea and ordered Miller's lawyers to proceed with their case.

While waiting to hear about whether Svetlana would be granted immunity against further prosecution so that she could be called as a defense witness, Miller's legal team made a crucial decision. After his shambling, somewhat incoherent performance during the trial of Svetlana and Nikolai, Greenberg and Levine had debated about putting Miller on the stand in his own trial. Now they decided it wasn't worth the risk. Instead, they chose to open their case by trying to prove that Miller really did have a plan to infiltrate the KGB. The defense called as its first witness Larry Grayson, the Riverside private investigator who had once paid Miller to supply him with inside information. Grayson was a reluctant witness, appearing under subpoena, and it took all of Stanley Greenberg's relentless grilling to get from him the details of a meeting with Miller at a Denny's Coffee Shop in Corona on August 15, 1984. Finally, Grayson told the court what he had already told the FBI — that Miller asked him to take pictures of him with "individuals of Russian nationality" at a meeting in Mexico that coming October. Grayson said he was ready to proceed, but that Miller never followed up on that initial request.

FBI Director William Webster was also involved in the trial. He had given an interview in Washington to the Scripps-Howard News Service that caused Miller's lawyers to issue a subpoena for him to testify as a defense witness. What Webster said was that FBI double agents are keeping the Soviets off balance and exposing their principal agents. "I think by maintaining a substantial counterintelligence campaign against known Soviet intelligence operations through the use of double agents, we're identifying and compromising their principal intelligence agents over here, intelligence agents who will work with us," Webster said in his interview. "We're also causing them to be suspicious of people who are offering information, because they don't know whether that's a bona fide traitor or an FBI agent." Miller's lawyers saw Webster's words as a chance to refute John Barron's testimony that the FBI would never use its own agents to penetrate a hostile intelligence operation such as the KGB. But the FBI chief managed to get the subpoena quashed, so his statement never got to the jury.

The Mormon Connection was brought up by the defense again, this time during a special hearing before Judge Kenyon with the jury absent. Bernardo (Matt) Perez, formerly the second-ranking FBI agent in the Los Angeles office and now in charge of the El Paso office, told Judge Kenyon in no uncertain terms that he had been prevented by Richard T. Bretzing from firing Miller in December of 1982 because Miller was a Mormon. Perez, a Roman Catholic who subsequently filed a religious discrimination complaint against Bretzing, said he was told to let Bryce Christensen handle Miller. "This was favored treatment in my opinion," Perez testified. "I think it was done because they were both Mormons." Perez's testimony was the cause of a heated exchange between Bonner and Greenberg — the latter charging that the Government had ordered Perez not to communicate directly with the defense, and Bonner countering that the charge was "piffled bombast." Judge Kenyon subsequently let the jury hear most of Perez's charges, but cut Greenberg off when he tried to raise the Mormon issue.

151

Two of Miller's former FBI supervisors took the stand for the defense and seemed to disprove the prosecution's claim that Miller never really knew how much trouble he was in at work until 1984. Retired agent Homer Porter, Miller's supervisor from 1974 to 1976, told the court that "R.W.'s work was like a roller coaster. He would start off doing good work for a while, and then he would slide off again. I cussed him out," Porter testified, when Miller lost an airline ticket and failed to submit travel vouchers. "Was anyone else present when you did this?" Stanley Greenberg asked. "Well, I usually talked loud enough for everyone in the office to hear," Porter replied.

Another former supervisor, William Scruggs, testified about receiving reports from other agents in 1980 that Miller was selling Amway products over the phone during working hours. Scruggs said that Miller was in "the lower third of the agents I supervised," and told the court that he once suggested that the FBI consider dismissing him. "I talked to Miller about every bad memo placed in his file," Scruggs said, when asked if it was possible that Miller could not have known he was in trouble.

On October 6, the defense rested, after first failing to get a key tape introduced as evidence. On the tape, made the day of his arrest a year before, Miller was heard talking on the telephone to his wife, Paula. Sounding like he was crying, Miller said on the tape, "I did some awfully dumb things, but I don't think I did what they think I did. The recollections are very foggy. I'm sure these guys think I'm the best bullshit artist this side of the Atlantic Ocean, but it just ain't true. I don't have anybody to turn to. I'm upside down and inside out. The more I review this in my own mind, the more I think I'm digging my own grave. I'm helping them hang me. As much as I want to cooperate, I don't want to spend the rest of my life in the slammer for something I don't think I did. I honestly believe I'm innocent. I don't remember knowingly passing documents. The allegation is life in prison; if they can prove in a court of law that I did what I did, then that's what the sentence is."

Miller's lawyers played the tape for Judge Kenyon with the jury absent. After hearing it, Judge Kenyon ruled that it should be excluded from evidence, saying it was made while Miller knew his conversations were being taped by the FBI. "It's a situation where he's talking with his wife with full knowledge he's being listened to and that everything he says is being taped," Judge Kenyon explained. "It would be a self-serving statement, with no chance to cross-examine."

Just before both sides began their closing arguments, the jurors got a break and an outing — a bus ride from the Federal Court downtown to the Little League parking lot just south of the Federal Building in Westwood, where Miller and Svetlana had so many meetings. The purpose of the trip was for the judge and jury to see for themselves if Miller could have recognized another FBI agent, Paul DeFlores, seated in his car about forty feet away. "He stepped out of his car and looked right at me and I looked at him," DeFlores later told his FBI superiors, describing Miller's look of "shock."

It was this moment of recognition that the prosecution claimed sent Miller into a flurry of confession on the next day. The defense said it never happened — that with the sun in his face Miller couldn't possibly have seen or recognized DeFlores. Each juror stood next to a car similar to Miller's to see if they could recognize the FBI staffer sitting in for DeFlores. They also took turns sitting in the driver's seat of the FBI car, to see if DeFlores would have been able to spot Miller getting out of Svetlana's car and notice the expression of "shock" on Miller's face. Judge Kenyon then told the jurors that the overcast skies made the viewing different today than on September 26, 1984. "We tried to wait for an absolutely similar day, a sunny day," Judge Kenyon said. "It's not as close today as we ideally would have liked."

Both sides began summing up their cases on October 15. Russell Hayman first outlined the Government's evidence, charging that it proved beyond a doubt that Miller had conspired with Nikolai and Svetlana to pass FBI documents to the Soviet KGB. Then came Joel Levine, who said that Miller had never passed any documents to Svetlana — he only admitted to doing so because he was emotionally and physically drained after five days of interrogation. He described Miller once again as a "bumbler" who should never have been placed on the counterintelligence squad. "The FBI knew before Mr. Miller ever met Svetlana Ogorodnikova on May 24, 1984, that he had been excommunicated from the Mormon Church for adultery, and that he faced dismissal from his job because of a chronic weight problem," Levine told the jury. "Yet, as of May 24, there seemed to be no lights going off to tell the FBI that Richard Miller was a classically recruitable agent. Why didn't somebody figure that out?"

Levine then talked about two of Miller's FBI colleagues who had testified against him. "John Hunt is not on trial," he said. "Richard Bretzing is not on trial. But their judgment is on trial. Their expertise is on trial."

With Miller's wife and two of their children looking on, Levine concluded his summation by saying, "The predominant issue in the case is what Mr. Miller's intent was in the summer of 1984. Was he intending to be a spy, or was he intending to be a double agent? I urge you to judge the matter on the facts of the case, and to give Mr. Miller the benefit of reasonable doubt. If you feel that Richard Miller intended to be a spy in the summer of 1984, he does not deserve your sympathy. If you feel that the evidence does not substantiate that charge, he doesn't need your sympathy."

Robert Bonner took off from Levine's comments about Hunt and Bretzing in his final statement. "The FBI is not on trial in this case. The only person on trial is right there — Richard W. Miller, that's the man on trial. What you've seen in this case is what you see in any case investigated by the FBI — fine men and women doing their job, in bitter contrast to that man right there." His voice rising in anger, Bonner responded to defense claims that Miller had been trying to help his country. "Quite frankly, I don't think Mr. Miller ever gave a second thought to his country," Bonner told the jury. "That's one of the most preposterous defenses that I've ever heard put forward to a jury. Mr. Miller disgraced and dishonored himself. By his conduct, he besmirched the name of the FBI and every loyal and dedicated agent who ever took the oath. The stain that Mr. Miller put on the FBI will dim in time, but it's never going to be erased."

Judge Kenyon sent the case to the jury on October 16, after two hours of instruction about espionage laws,

155

criminal intent, and exactly what they had to believe if they were to find Miller guilty on each of the counts against him. In the light of the jury tampering charges that had just been raised in the bribery case against San Diego Mayor Roger Hedgecock, Judge Kenyon also issued a stern warning to the jurors against becoming overly friendly with bailiffs.

Two weeks later, after seventy-one hours of deliberation, the six men and six women came back with some startling news. They were deadlocked 10–2 for conviction on three of the seven counts against Miller, and 11–1 for conviction on the other four counts. "Miller was browbeaten and swayed by the interrogation by the FBI," one holdout juror later said. "He would have signed anything put in front of him. The only evidence saying he was guilty was when he admitted passing documents. That was the only incriminating evidence, and we felt that it was made under mental duress. He was interrogated ten, twelve, fourteen hours a day. That's why we two felt his admission of guilt was not valid." The two holdout jurors also believed Miller's story about trying to use Svetlana to infiltrate the KGB and save his job. "We felt he was doing it for the FBI," one of them said, adding that he and his fellow holdout believed the FBI had suppressed some of the evidence pointing in that direction.

The same juror said that the Miller jury took sides early in the deliberations, and then "wouldn't budge. People walked in with their minds made up. We briefly discussed a deal in which the holdouts would vote guilty on some counts in exchange for innocent verdicts on other counts, but then we decided that kind of horse trading wouldn't be ethical." The jury first told Judge Kenyon that it was deadlocked on Friday, November 1; he asked them to forget about the case over the weekend and begin deliberations again on Monday. Shortly after noon on Wednesday, the jury sent Judge Kenyon a note saying they were hopelessly deadlocked, and that further efforts would be futile. Kenyon questioned the jurors individually; some thought they might eventually agree on a verdict, but most felt it would never happen. U.S. Attorney Bonner asked Judge Kenyon to order the jury to resume their deliberations, but Kenyon turned down his request and declared a mistrial on November 6, 1985. Bonner announced that he would immediately ask for another trial of Miller, on all counts. Defense attorneys said they planned to file a motion for acquittal. "It's a defeat for the Government, but not a victory for Mr. Miller," Stanley Greenberg said, as his client — wearing a gray three-piece suit and red tie — stood silent. "Mr. Miller is still in jail."

Chapter 11

THE SECOND TIME AROUND

Were Miller's trysts with the lovely Svetlana only for sexual pleasure, or did he use the bedroom as a means to pass her "secret" U.S. documents? He said it was for pleasure. On the witness stand, she agreed. The jury did not!

B Y February of 1986, it was time for the next act of this long-running legal drama: the second trial of Richard Miller. Both sides had learned a lot from the first trial, even though Judge Kenyon's ongoing gag order kept them from talking about it until later. The Government took extra care to keep people who worked in the mental health and social services area off the jury. (The two holdouts in the first trial had jobs in those fields.) The reason Svetlana hadn't been used as a prosecution witness in the first trial, it came out through court papers, was that she had failed a lie detector test. So she wouldn't be called by the Government this time either, although at first they didn't seem to mind if the defense used her. The prosecution also thought hard about postponing or limiting John Hunt's testimony, because it had been the subject of the most scrutiny by the previous jury. As for the defense, now that Svetlana had been granted immunity against further prosecution, they decided to build their case around her testimony and still keep Miller himself off the stand.

160

PHOTO:THE NEW RUSSIAN WORD DAILY (RUSSIAN LANGUAGE NEWSPAPER)

On February 25, in front of a jury of ten women and two men, U.S. Attorney Robert Bonner once again outlined the case for the prosecution in his opening statement. He portrayed Miller as a man disgruntled with his work and mired in financial and marital problems — a "classic target" for recruitment by Soviet spies. The trial would probably last eight to ten weeks, Bonner told the jury, "during which time you'll learn much about the world of espionage. The evidence will show that it's not glamorous like spy novels or television. It's a much grimier, more sordid reality. There's nothing glamorous about it. I don't think you'll find that Richard Miller is anything like Efrem Zimbalist, Jr.," the star of the TV series *The FBI*. Bonner listed some of the evidence against Miller: surveillance reports and video and audio tapes of his meetings with his Soviet contacts. He used charts to show on what dates various events took place as he ran down the list of contacts between Miller and Svetlana from May to October of 1984.

"The Government will prove that Miller was pursuing his own venal interests, his own sexual interests, not the interests of the FBI," he told the jury. "We do not believe we have to prove an intent to betray or injure the United States, because that is not charged in any of the counts. But when all the evidence is added up, you will see how Richard Miller sold out his country." Stanley Greenberg made it clear that John Hunt was one of the defense's main targets in his opening statement. "There is no question that in the summer of 1982, Svetlana Ogorodnikova fell in love with John Hunt and he took advantage of her," he told the jury. "Bonner claims that Hunt maintained contact with her after that first proposition of sex in June of 1982. You want to know how many times he maintained contact? Fifty-five to sixty in the next one hundred and twenty days!" Greenberg also claimed that it was Hunt who introduced Svetlana to Miller. When her call came to the FBI office in August of 1984, Greenberg said, "it was another agent who took the call and handed it to Miller, saying, 'Here, R.W., it's for you.' We believe that other agent to be John Hunt, although we don't expect him to admit it."

The evidence would show that Miller wasn't venal or a traitor, Greenberg continued, just "an overweight Inspector Clouseau who bumbled and fumbled his way through the FBI for twenty years — a grown man who entertained fantasies of being James Bond. He's done a lot of bad, stupid, and dumb things in his life, but he's not on trial for any of those," Greenberg said. "What he's accused of is espionage." Greenberg added that no U.S. documents had been passed to Russia through Mr. Miller, and warned, "In this case, nothing looks like what is."

The first batch of prosecution witnesses were familiar to watchers of the earlier trials: café owner Mischa Makarian, Russian émigré Gregory Shenderovsky, defector's wife Karine Matevossian. Then, on March 11, came a voice from the grave. The testimony which Ludmilla Kondratjeva had given at Miller's first trial — about being introduced to the FBI agent by her friend Svetlana — was read to the jury by a court stenographer. Kondratjeva herself was found dead in the Pacific off Malibu three days after Christmas, strangled by her boyfriend.

Throughout the rest of March and on into April, the Government presented essentially the same case it had

163

laid out before. Marta York repeated her story about Miller's telephone "confession"; security experts such as retired Gen. Richard A. Larkin and author John Barron talked about their areas of expertise; dozens of FBI agents told the jury about Miller's surveillance and his admissions during their grillings. John Hunt finally appeared, and despite objections from the prosecution (who wanted to limit his testimony to 1984) was made to testify about events from 1982 onward. He told essentially the same story he had already told twice, and when he was done the prosecution rested its case. Then, on April 22, Miller's second trial took a dramatic turn, as defense witness Svetlana Ogorodnikova took the stand for the first time and began what would be seven full days of amazing testimony.

Small and vulnerable-looking in prison khaki, her voice husky, she started slowly, talking about her film business and the way she used false visa information to go back and forth to Russia. She segued into her relationship with John Hunt, which, despite his denials, she insisted was a sexual one. "When he ask me to work for him, he ask me personal, like a friend," she said about her role as an FBI informant. "I answer him like a friend. Later, when I was arrested and saw the things he write, I don't believe it. He lie. I am not try to help Russia. I don't believe I am involved in those things." She also said that Hunt had once paid for her to have an abortion.

Two days later, first in an emotional scene in Judge Kenyon's chambers and then in court with the jury absent, Svetlana took back the entire confession she had made when she entered her guilty plea in June of 1985. "Your honor, we are not guilty of this crime," a sobbing

Svetlana told the judge. "Richard is not a traitor to his country. I am not a spy. I was helping the American government. That is true, Your Honor. We are not guilty of this crime." Svetlana then spoke of an "FBI plan from Washington" that had involved her with Miller. "Someday you will know who drafted that plan. My hands are clean. I not take no documents," she went on, directly contradicting her earlier confession. "I help America, not Russia." On one of her trips back to Russia, she told Judge Kenyon, she was beaten in her mother's village by KGB agents because "I think they understood I was working with the FBI."

Asked by Judge Kenyon why she had pleaded guilty last year, Svetlana blamed it on pressure from her attorneys. "When I was arrested, I couldn't understand anything. My lawyers say because I am Russian, they would give me life sentence. They told me no one would believe me — the judge would maybe give me forty years. I plead guilty; my life is finished anyway. If I go back to Soviet Union, they kill me."

She said she had begun to change her mind about the confession almost immediately, when she looked out into the courtroom last June and saw Richard Miller's son, Drew. "When I saw his son, his face, I thought that could be my son, Matthew could be in his place. I want to tell his son, 'Your father is not guilty.' But I was scared. I am Russian. . . the jury would not believe me." Then, during her first days of testimony in the current trial, her conscience began to bother her; she couldn't sleep. "I didn't want someone who is not guilty to be in prison. Richard lie a lot about me, but it's not his fault. He is very emotional man. The truth has to come out, and the person who is not guilty should not be charged.

165

I ask also for my husband. They know that we're not guilty. The FBI knows. Mr. Bonner knows."

Back on the witness stand the next day, under questioning from Stanley Greenberg, Svetlana insisted that Miller was a good, hard-working FBI agent who repeatedly pestered her to give him information about Soviet officials, promising that she would be well paid. "He had an emotional stress," she testified. "He could not concentrate, and he said that if I could help and give him this information, it would help his career."

"At any time during your relationship with Mr. Miller were you in love with him?" asked Greenberg.

"I cannot say that I was in love with him," Svetlana replied. "But he's a nice man."

Frequently breaking into sobs or sniffles, Svetlana told the court that she was drunk during most of the time she spent with Miller, and remembered very little about what happened. "All those days, all those months, I was drunk — too drunk. And I was taking some pills," she said. She also denied ever having seen any of the classified documents that Miller claimed to have shown her at his Lynwood house. Greenberg was quick to read into the record an FBI report which stated that none of the fingerprints on the documents were hers.

Most of her fifth day on the stand was spent discussing John Hunt rather than Richard Miller. She spoke about her trip to Moscow in June of 1984, and said a KGB agent gave her instructions about Hunt — not Miller, as the prosecution claimed. "He told me, 'Svetlana, could you invite your friend Mr. Hunt somewhere for a trip abroad in Europe?' I said I would try."

Prodded by Greenberg as to whether the KGB agent had also mentioned Miller, she answered angrily, "How could I tell him anything about Miller when we were talking only about Hunt?"

She went on to say that she met with both Hunt and Miller several times when she got back from Russia, but she was so drunk during the meetings that she couldn't recall any details. She said that Miller used to identify himself as "Pedro" or "Boris" when he called and Nikolai answered the phone. "Once Miller asked me if someone from Soviet Union knew how Hunt looked," she told the court. "I said no. He asked me to help him contact Russians. Always it was the same."

Testifying again that she had never delivered any documents from Miller to the Soviet Consulate, Svetlana characterized their trip to San Francisco in August of 1984 as nothing more than a weekend of pleasure. "We just went to have a good time," she told the court. Then she indicated that she had been aware of Miller's plan to use her to infiltrate the KGB, although Miller never said that he told her of his intentions. "He say he want to make the Russians think he work for them," she told a surprised-looking Greenberg. Svetlana ended her seven days of direct testimony by swearing once again — this time in front of the jury — that she and Miller were innocent.

"The FBI knows we're not guilty, and the prosecution knows," she sobbed softly. "He did not give me any documents. I did no harm to America. How can I explain? We were talking two different languages." Asked again why she had pleaded guilty, she replied, "I had no other choice. When I was arrested, everybody was lying — Miller because he was in shock and I because I was drunk. I saw that everyone was against me. I lost my friends, my family, the country I betrayed. Who would help me? I asked my lawyers about the situation: could I win or lose? There was only more losing. I couldn't fight anymore. My chance is life sentence — for what? So I decided to plead guilty."

As she completed her testimony, Svetlana dropped one more potential bomb on Miller's defense and barely dodged a land mine. She told the jury she might have tipped off Miller that they were being followed by the FBI in September of 1984, when she wrote down the license number of a suspicious car and gave it him. And when she was asked if she knew that John Hunt had had a vasectomy several years before she claimed he paid for her to have an abortion, Svetlana answered quickly, "I never accused him. I just told him I was pregnant after I went to see the doctor."

Then it was the prosecution's turn to blast away at Svetlana for another six days. Russell Hayman began by trying to get her to admit that she was protecting KGB agents in America in case Russia made a bid for a possible swap for her later on. She seemed not to understand the questions, so Hayman moved on to whether or not her repudiation of her confession and her attempt to get Miller acquitted had anything to do with helping Nikolai get a new trial. "I cannot say," she replied to this. "I don't know if Miller is acquitted it will help my husband." Hayman concluded his cross-examination by trying to get Svetlana to admit that she had lied about her relationship with John Hunt.

"When you told this jury that John Hunt took you to the doctor, weren't you trying to lead them to believe that he had made you pregnant?" Hayman asked. "No," Svetlana answered. "You backed off that claim, didn't you, when the defense suggested to you that John Hunt had had a vasectomy?" "I did not talk to the lawyers," she replied.

"You blame John Hunt more than anyone for the fact that you've been convicted, don't you?" Hayman continued.

"I don't blame anybody," Svetlana said. "I blame myself. But I wouldn't be sitting here if it wasn't for John Hunt."

Svetlana had been the defense's chief witness, and when she was finished they rested their case. Almost immediately, Hayman rose again to begin the Government's closing statement.

"Svetlana Ogorodnikova is an admitted liar under oath," he told the jury. "She first testified under oath that she had taken documents into the Soviet Consulate, and then she said under oath that she had lied. Because she is an admitted liar under oath, you are entitled to reject her testimony outright. The Government suggests you do precisely that. Svetlana was on the stand for three long weeks, as I'm sure you remember, and she lied to you day after day."

Pointing out that other witnesses had contradicted her on virtually every aspect of her testimony, Hayman continued, "Svetlana was willing to lie to you whenever necessary to avoid incriminating her husband and Richard Miller. Her lies about Nikolai are so extreme that she characterized her husband as a beautiful, loving man, although testimony from other witnesses is that he beat her and that she hated him."

Joel Levine hammered away at the issue of documents passed or not passed in his closing statement for the defense. "The only evidence the prosecution has that Richard Miller ever gave Svetlana Ogorodnikova any documents are his own words to the FBI, given under extreme pressure," Levine told the jury. "The FBI and the prosecution are trying to convict him with speculation disguised as proof. The true test is whether there is any independent evidence that these acts took place. In fact, there is no evidence that a document ever passed between them."

As the prosecution took its last crack at Miller, Robert Bonner denied that any of Miller's admissions to his FBI questioners were the result of undue pressure. "Miller was free to leave the office any time he wanted to during the questioning," Bonner told the jury. "And in fact he did so on October 2, to make a telephone call to Marta York. You'll recall that when she asked him if he had passed any documents to the Russians, he told her, 'I only did one.'"

When Bonner remarked that the jury should remember Miller chose not to appear on the witness stand himself, Stanley Greenberg angrily leaped to his feet to demand a mistrial. Judge Kenyon denied the motion; another angry outburst brought Greenberg a $500 fine for contempt of court. Bonner quickly wrapped up his closing statement; then Judge Kenyon gave the jury his instructions and ordered them to begin their deliberations on June 16.

The end came a lot faster the second time around. After chewing it over for a total of twenty-one hours during the next four days, the jury came back on June 19 with a verdict of guilty on six of the seven counts. The only one they couldn't agree on was the bribery count involving the $675 Burberry, so Bonner quickly moved to have that charge dismissed. He also asked Judge Kenyon to lift his gag order, and when that was done the jurors were free to talk openly about why they convicted Miller. Most of them said that Svetlana's testimony had been too much to swallow. "Ninety-eight percent of it I just couldn't believe," said one man. "There were just too many contradictions." The foreman said that everyone was baffled by Svetlana. "We thought that in some instances she may have been telling the truth, but the rest of the evidence outweighed anything she said." Jurors also were swayed by the fact that Miller didn't testify, as well as by the confessions he made to the FBI. "We had the easiest time with his own admissions," said one. Added another, "The most difficult thing was his motive, but we finally concluded it was mostly for his own gain."

Miller's only comment to reporters, as he was led away in handcuffs, was, "Let's just say, Thank God for the Court of Appeals." He was back in court on July 14, and before Judge Kenyon sentenced him he finally had the chance — still against his lawyers' advice — to say a few words in his own defense. Miller began with an attack on the justice system: "Your honor, to paraphrase a wise observer who said something like this, 'There are many who seek to administer justice, but few who are able to do it.' I have some stuff to present. I never intended to injure this country or benefit the Soviet Union. My conduct did no damage to this country. I know you are going to sentence me as if I did commit these crimes, but I did not commit them. I will continue to assert my innocence through the appellate process, which I hope will result in a new and fair trial."

Unmoved, Judge Kenyon called Miller a "tormented man" and sentenced him to two life terms plus fifty years in prison as well as $60,000 in fines. "This case has been a tremendous lesson to the court," Kenyon said. "As a boy, my mother used to constantly refer to my being grateful when I complained about some things. The fundamental trouble Miller had was he did not appreciate that. Because he had everything. He had eight children he helped bring into this world, the privilege of watching them grow. He had a wife who stuck by him. He had his church. He had superiors in the FBI whom he resented, but he should have been very grateful for the way they treated him. He had a position of respect and a rare opportunity of service to his government. If Mr. Miller had been grateful for any one of those things, he would not be here today. My heart goes out to Mr. Miller, because my impression is that he is a tormented man. We are all here to learn a lesson, because that's what life is about. A man without gratitude has to be a tormented men."

Chapter 12

FROM BLACK CANYON

A FEW weeks after Judge Kenyon's verdict and sermon, Terminal Island lost two prisoners. Early on the morning of July 30, 1986, Richard Miller was whisked away to a small Federal prison in Rochester, Minnesota. His former wife, Paula, who had filed for divorce the previous November but who continued to visit him regularly with their children, complained he had been moved so quickly and secretly that there had been no chance to say good-bye. Miller popped up two months later on the television program *60 Minutes*, bloated and sad and foolish. (On the same program, Svetlana looked glamorous and sounded certifiably insane at her current home, the Federal prison in Pleasanton, California.)

Shortly before Miller was moved, Nikolai Ogorod-nikov — the forgotten man in the case, never mentioned on *60 Minutes* — also got a new address. "They keep me in Terminal Island for a year so I can testify in the Miller trial," he says. "And then they never call me!" Nikolai was finally transferred to Black Canyon, a Federal facility outside of Phoenix, Arizona. He has a job making uniforms — a trade he has adapted to as quickly as he once took up meat cutting. While he waits for his appeal to wend its way through the legal system, he has plenty of time to think about the past and the future.

"I can hardly remember what Svetlana was like when I first met her," he says. "There I was, almost a middle-aged man, divorced, with a kid. She was no more than a kid herself, from a provincial village in Tula, just out of school, working as an assistant janitor in an apartment building in Kiev. But even from the start, I noticed that my young bride was attracted to alcohol. Later, as I say, I heard that her father was also an alcoholic, and this had contributed to his early death. Should I have tried to get her treatment, or at least kept a better watch on her? Probably yes, I admit it.

"Did I ever hit her, as they said at the trial? Yes, it's true. I sometimes lost my temper. Not long before we were arrested, it was a weekend day, Matthew was playing outside and I was sitting on the sofa. The phone rang in the next room, and I heard Svetlana apparently talking to a woman friend. Then, after about ten minutes, she began cursing loudly — the most awful words. On and on she went. Finally, I couldn't stand it; I took the phone from her hands and gave her a big smack on the ear. She was yelling as loud as she could, I hit her twice more, she took a kitchen knife and tried to use it on me but I wrestled it away from her and threw her down on the coach. She cried for a while, then fell asleep — the usual pattern for a violent alcoholic.

"There were other arguments, but what I must mention is that in other ways Svetlana was never a very passionate woman. That's why I was surprised by all the sex things she did. I think she was looking for adventure, romance — not sex.

"About a year before our arrest, I threatened Svetlana that if she didn't stop doing the nasty business of the Soviet Consulate, if she continued to spend her evenings and nights in bars and restaurants, if she didn't start looking after Matthew, I was going to write a letter to the authorities and tell them everything I knew. I might not get off myself, but I would at least have a cleaner conscience. The threat worked — for a while. She stopped seeing her friends, stayed home at night and kept the apartment clean. Every night there was dinner on the table: she remembered my favorite dishes, like Ukrainian borscht, chicken soup with dumplings, sweet and sour stew. Our life seemed to be getting back to normal.

"Then, one day at noon, she called me at work and told me she had been invited to see the opening of a new film, and that she would be home about 11 P.M. Needless to say, she returned at dawn, her hair and eyes wild, her voice loud and drunken. I knew somehow that this slip was for keeps.

"Aside from the drinking, why did she do it — what was she looking for in the spy business? I've asked myself that question a thousand times. I think she felt like a fish in the wrong water, never part of America but not fully accepted by the other Russians, either. John Hunt and the FBI first took advantage of that; they promised her love and being part of a team; so did Grishin and the KGB. The trouble was, she never knew which team she was really on. By the time Miller came along, she had messed up badly for both sides. The more I think about it, the more I believe that Miller was as much a chance for Svetlana to prove herself to the KGB as she was for him to show the FBI what he could do. Each was using the other, and both got hurt. And others on the sidelines also got hurt. Not only me, but our son, and Miller's family.

"Even if my appeal doesn't get heard, I am still eligible for parole in 1987. I'll have been in jail over two years by then. What will I do if I get paroled? Go back to Los Angeles, of course — that's my home now. Get some kind of job again. They liked me at the meat plant, and some of the people have written to say I'd be welcome back. Most of all, bring my son back to me. He is with his grandmother, Svetlana's mother, in Russia now, but he has a return ticket to Los Angeles.

"Will Svetlana join us when she gets out? I can't say at all for certain right now. We write to each other, but we've never really had the chance to talk about what happened to us. I don't know if you can ever get over something like that."